PRESTWICK HOUSE, INC.

KING LEAR

WILLIAM SHAKESPEARE

Shakespeare's text

on the left;

a modern rendering

on the right.

Prestwick House

P.O. Box 658 • Clayton, DE 19938
Tel: 1.800.932.4593
Web site: www.prestwickhouse.com

ISBN 978-1-58049-512-7

— summarize every 2 pages or 5 pages

— Annotate acc to Mrs. Proctor feedback . . .

— Read Daily + Balance w/ BOC.

— participate in forums by wed + thurs
                                   at latest.

Table of Contents

.DO STUDY GUIDE!
BY

4

DRAMATIS PERSONAE

LEAR King of Britain

KING OF FRANCE

DUKE OF BURGUNDY

DUKE OF CORNWALL

DUKE OF ALBANY

EARL OF KENT

EARL OF GLOUCESTER

EDGAR son to GLOUCESTER

EDMUND illegitimate son to GLOUCESTER

CURAN a courtier

OLD MAN tenant to GLOUCESTER

DOCTOR

FOOL

OSWALD steward to GONERIL

A Captain employed by EDMUND

Gentleman attending on CORDELIA

A Herald

Servants to CORNWALL

GONERIL
REGAN } daughters to LEAR
CORDELIA

Knights of LEAR'S train, Captains, Messengers, Soldiers, and Attendants.

ACT I

SCENE I

King Lear's palace.

[Enter Kent, Gloucester, and Edmund]

KENT: I thought the king had <u>more affected</u> the Duke of
Albany than Cornwall. *favored*

GLOUCESTER: It did always seem so to us: but now, in the division of
the kingdom, it appears not which of the dukes he values most;
5   for equalities are so weighed, that curiosity in neither can make
choice of either's moiety.

KENT: Is not this your son, my lord?

Being his father   *been my responsibility*

GLOUCESTER: His breeding, sir, hath been at my charge: I have so
often blushed to acknowledge him, that now I am brazed to it.
ashamed

10 KENT: I cannot conceive you.
understand

GLOUCESTER: Sir, this young fellow's mother could: whereupon she
grew round-wombed, and had, indeed, sir, a son for her cradle
ere she had a husband for her bed. Do you smell a fault?
gave birth before seeing her husband

KENT: I cannot wish the fault undone, the issue of it being so
15   proper.

6

ACT I

SCENE I

King Lear's palace.

[Kent, Gloucester, and Edmund enter]

KENT: *I thought the king favored the Duke of Albany over the Duke of Cornwall.*

GLOUCESTER: *It always seemed that way to us. But the division of the kingdom does not reveal which of the dukes he values most. Their shares have been divided equally, so that neither is preferred to the other.*

KENT: *Isn't this your son, my lord?*

GLOUCESTER: *Fathering him, Sir, has been my responsibility. I have often been ashamed to acknowledge him, but now I am used to it.*

KENT: *I don't understand you.*

GLOUCESTER: *Sir, this young man's mother could! She became pregnant and gave birth to a son before she even had a husband. Do you sense a fault?*

KENT: *I can't wish the mistake undone, for the outcome is so handsome.*

GLOUCESTER: But I have, sir, a son by order of law, some year elder
than this, who yet is no dearer in my account: though this
knave came something saucily into the world before he was sent
for, yet was his mother fair; there was good sport at his making,
20   and the whoreson must be acknowledged. Do you know this
noble gentleman, Edmund?

EDMUND: No, my lord.

GLOUCESTER: My lord of Kent: remember him hereafter as my
honourable friend.

25   EDMUND: My services to your lordship.

KENT: I must love you, and sue to know you better.

beg

EDMUND: Sir, I shall study deserving.

try to be worthy of your acquaintance

GLOUCESTER: He hath been out nine years, and away he shall again.
The king is coming. *been abroad.*

[Sennet. Enter KING LEAR, CORNWALL, ALBANY, GONERIL, REGAN, CORDELIA,
and Attendants]

30   KING LEAR: Attend the lords of France and Burgundy, Gloucester.

GLOUCESTER: I shall, my liege.   [Exeunt GLOUCESTER and EDMUND]

KING LEAR: Meantime we shall express our darker purpose.
Give me the map there. Know that we have divided
In three our kingdom: and 'tis our fast intent
To shake all cares and business from our age;
35   Conferring them on younger strengths, while we

*King lear has secret plan to divide kingdom into 3 parts
then overturn throne.*

8

GLOUCESTER: *But, sir, I also have a legitimate son, about a year older than this one, whom I don't favor. Although this young fellow slipped into the world before he was sent for, his mother was beautiful, and we had fun producing him, so he must be recognized as my son. Do you know this noble gentleman, Edmund?*

EDMUND: *No, my Lord.*

GLOUCESTER: *This is the lord of Kent. Remember him from now on as my honorable friend.*

EDMUND: *I am at your service, my lordship.*

KENT: *I must love you and beg to know you better.*

EDMUND: *Sir, I will try to be worthy of your acquaintance.*

GLOUCESTER: *He has been abroad for nine years, and he will leave again. The king is coming.*

[A trumpet plays signaling the arrival of a procession. A Servant carrying a coronet enters, followed by King Lear, Cornwall, Albany, Goneril, Regan, Cordelia, and Attendants of the royal court]

KING LEAR: *Bring in the lords of France and Burgundy, Gloucester.*

GLOUCESTER: *I will, my lord.*

[Gloucester and Edmund exit]

KING LEAR: *In the meantime, we will reveal our secret plan. Give me the map there. Know that I have divided my kingdom into three parts, and that it is my serious intention to give up all matters of business, at my approaching age, and hand them over to the younger and stronger generation, while I, relieved of any*

Unburthen'd crawl toward death. Our son of Cornwall,
And you, our no less loving son of Albany,
We have this hour a constant will to publish
40 Our daughters' several dowers, that future strife
May be prevented now. The princes, France and Burgundy,
Great rivals in our youngest daughter's love,
Long in our court have made their amorous sojourn,
And here are to be answer'd. Tell me, my daughters,—
45 Since now we will divest us both of rule,
Interest of territory, cares of state,—
Which of you shall we say doth love us most?
That we our largest bounty may extend
Where nature doth with merit challenge. Goneril,
50 Our eldest-born, speak first.

prince of France + Burgundy at war for king Lear's daughter's love.

GONERIL: Sir, I love you more than words can wield the matter;
Dearer than eye-sight, space, and liberty;
Beyond what can be valued, rich or rare;
No less than life, with grace, health, beauty, honour;
55 As much as child e'er loved, or father found;
A love that makes breath poor, and speech unable;
Beyond all manner of so much I love you.

CORDELIA: [Aside] What shall Cordelia do? Love, and be silent.

LEAR: Of all these bounds, even from this line to this,
60 With shadowy forests and with champains rich'd,
With plenteous rivers and wide-skirted meads,
We make thee lady: to thine and Albany's issue
Be this perpetual. What says our second daughter,
Our dearest Regan, wife to Cornwall? Speak.

65 REGAN: Sir, I am made
Of the self-same metal that my sister is,
And prize me at her worth. In my true heart

10

burdens, prepare for death. My son-in-law of Cornwall and my equally loving son-in-law of Albany: at this moment, I intend to publicly announce my daughters' individual dowries, so that future conflict can be prevented. The two princes, the prince of France and the prince of Burgundy, great rivals for the favor of my youngest daughter, have resided at my court as suitors for a while, and I will answer them today. Tell me, my daughters, since I will distance myself today from leadership, territorial possessions, and cares of state, which of you shall we say loves me most? Then we can give the largest inheritance to the one who deserves it by nature as well as worthiness. Goneril, our oldest daughter, speak first.

GONERIL: Sir, I love you more than words can express. I love you more than eyesight, freedom, and independence. More than anything valuable or rare, more than life itself filled with grace, health, beauty, and honor. I love you more than any child ever loved a father, and I give more love than any father ever received. My love makes my voice weak and my speaking difficult. More than all I have said, I love you.

CORDELIA: [Aside] What shall Cordelia say? Love, and then be silent.

KING LEAR: The area between these boundaries, from this line to that line, full of shadowy forests and open country, with plentiful rivers and broad meadows, shall be your territory. This will belong to you and your husband Albany's family forever. What does our second daughter, our dearest Regan, wife of the Duke of Cornwall, say? Speak.

REGAN: I am made of the same mettle as my sister and consider myself her equal when it comes to loving you. In my honest heart, I feel that she exactly describes my love for you. But she

I find she names my very deed of love;
Only she comes too short: that I profess
70   Myself an enemy to all other joys,
Which the most precious square of sense possesses;
And find I am alone felicitate
In your dear highness' love.

CORDELIA: *[Aside]* Then poor Cordelia!
75   And yet not so; since, I am sure, my love's
More richer than my tongue.

] my love is
   greater
than words can
   express.

KING LEAR: To thee and thine hereditary ever
Remain this ample third of our fair kingdom;
No less in space, validity, and pleasure,
80   Than that conferr'd on Goneril. Now, our joy,
Although the last, not least; to whose young love
The vines of France and milk of Burgundy
Strive to be interess'd; what can you say to draw
A third more opulent than your sisters? Speak.

85   CORDELIA: Nothing, my lord.

KING LEAR: Nothing!

CORDELIA: Nothing.

KING LEAR: Nothing will come of nothing: speak again.

CORDELIA: Unhappy that I am, I cannot heave
90   My heart into my mouth: I love your majesty
According to my bond; nor more nor less.

KING LEAR: How, how, Cordelia! mend your speech a little,
Lest it may mar your fortunes.

CORDELIA: Good my lord,
95   You have begot me, bred me, loved me: I

12

does not go far enough: I despise all other joys that the human body can sense. I can only find happiness in your love.

CORDELIA: [Aside] *Poor Cordelia! But not quite, since I am sure that my love is more profound than my words.*

KING LEAR: *This generous third of our beautiful kingdom shall belong to you and your family forever. It has no less space, value, and pleasing qualities than the part given to Goneril. Now, our joy, the last one born, but not the least, for whose young love the vineyards of France and the pastures of Burgundy compete in rivalry. What can you say in order to win a third part of land more magnificent than your sisters'? Speak!*

CORDELIA: *Nothing, my lord.*

KING LEAR: *Nothing.*

CORDELIA: *Nothing.*

KING LEAR: *Nothing will lead to nothing! Speak again.*

CORDELIA: *Unhappy as I am, I cannot express the feelings of my heart through words. I love your majesty according to my duty as your daughter; no more, no less.*

KING LEAR: *What, what, Cordelia. Correct your words, or they will ruin your fortunes!*

CORDELIA: *Good, my lord. You have fathered me, raised me, and*

Return those duties back as are right fit,
Obey you, love you, and most honour you.
Why have my sisters husbands, if they say
They love you all? Haply, when I shall wed,
100   That lord whose hand must take my plight shall carry
Half my love with him, half my care and duty:
Sure, I shall never marry like my sisters,
To love my father all.

her commitment + love to her father — only give half herself to her suitor

KING LEAR: But goes thy heart with this?

105   CORDELIA: Ay, good my lord.

KING LEAR: So young, and so untender?

CORDELIA: So young, my lord, and true.

KING LEAR: Let it be so; thy truth, then, be thy dower:
For, by the sacred radiance of the sun,
110   The mysteries of Hecate, and the night;
By all the operation of the orbs
From whom we do exist, and cease to be;
Here I disclaim all my paternal care, *→ he is not her father anymore.*
Propinquity and property of blood,
115   And as a stranger to my heart and me *she is now a stranger*
Hold thee, from this, for ever. The barbarous Scythian,
Or he that makes his generation messes
To gorge his appetite, shall to my bosom
Be as well neighbour'd, pitied, and relieved, *he despises his daughter now*
120   As thou my sometime daughter.

KENT: Good my liege,—

KING LEAR: Peace, Kent!
Come not between the dragon and his wrath.
I loved her most, and thought to set my rest
125   On her kind nursery. Hence, and avoid my sight!

angry at Kent for marrying her away from him.

14

loved me. I am appropriately dutiful in return. I obey you, love you, and honor you very much. Why do my sisters have husbands if they say they love only you? Surely, when I will marry, the man who receives my marriage promise will have half of my love, half of my care and duty. Certainly I'll never marry like my sisters did—and love only my father.

KING LEAR: Is this what you feel in your heart?

CORDELIA: Yes, my good lord.

KING LEAR: So young, and so insensitive?

CORDELIA: So young, my lord, and honest.

KING LEAR: That's how it will be. Your honesty will be your dowry. By the sacred beams of the sun, by the mysteries of Hecate, goddess of the moon and night, by the influence of the stars that determine life and death, I disclaim my fatherly care, my intimacy, and our blood relationship. From this day on forever, I will consider you a stranger to my heart and me! The barbarous inhabitants of Scythia or anyone who eats his children in order to satisfy his appetite will be as close to my heart, as pitied and comforted, as you, my former daughter.

KENT: But my lord—

KING LEAR: Be quiet, Kent! Don't come between the dragon and the object of his wrath. I loved her most of all and planned on retiring under her loving care. Go away, get out of my sight. My grave will be my resting place, as I take her father's love away from her.

So be my grave my peace, as here I give
Her father's heart from her! Call France; who stirs?
Call Burgundy. Cornwall and Albany,
With my two daughters' dowers digest this third:
130   Let pride, which she calls plainness, marry her.
I do invest you jointly with my power,
Pre-eminence, and all the large effects
That troop with majesty. Ourself, by monthly course,
With reservation of an hundred knights,
135   By you to be sustain'd, shall our abode
Make with you by due turns. Only we still retain
The name, and all the additions to a king;
The sway, revenue, execution of the rest,
Beloved sons, be yours: which to confirm,
140   This coronet part betwixt you.

KENT: Royal Lear,
Whom I have ever honour'd as my king,
Loved as my father, as my master follow'd,
As my great patron thought on in my prayers,—

145   KING LEAR: The bow is bent and drawn, make from the shaft. — *steal away from my rage*

KENT: Let it fall rather, though the fork invade
The region of my heart: be Kent unmannerly,
When Lear is mad. What wilt thou do, old man? *personification*
Think'st thou that duty shall have dread to speak, *of*
150   When power to flattery bows? To plainness honour's bound, *anger to*
When majesty stoops to folly. Reverse thy doom; *a bow &*
And, in thy best consideration, cheque *the arrow's*
This hideous rashness: answer my life my judgment, *path*
Thy youngest daughter does not love thee least;
155   Nor are those empty-hearted whose low sound
Reverbs no hollowness.

KING LEAR: Kent, on thy life, no more.

KENT: My life I never held but as a pawn

16

Call the prince of France. Quick. Call the prince of Burgundy. Call the Dukes of Cornwall and Albany. Divide the third part of land between the dowries of my two other daughters. Let pride, which she calls frankness, be her husband. I give you equal parts of my power, my supremacy, and all attributes associated with kingship. I myself, along with one hundred knights who will be maintained at your expense, will reside with each of you in turn for one month at a time. I will only retain the name and the honorary title of a king. The authority, profits, and administrative duties will be yours, my beloved sons-in-law. In confirmation, I divide this coronet between the two of you.

KENT: *Royal Lear, whom I've always honored as my king, loved as if he was my father, followed as my master, and prayed for as my patron—*

KING LEAR: *The bow is bent and drawn; stay out of its range!*

KENT: *Let it strike, then, even though the arrow will pierce my heart. I, Kent, must be disrespectful when Lear is mad. What are you doing, old man? Do you think that the dutiful will be afraid to speak when the powerful fall victim to flattery? Honor depends on honest words when his majesty descends into foolishness. Reconsider your decision and reflect on this dreadful haste. I risk my life for my opinion: Your youngest daughter doesn't love you least, nor are they heartless whose subtle words contain no insincerities.*

KING LEAR: *Kent, on your life, no more!*

KENT: *I have never viewed my life as anything other than a pledge to*

To wage against thy enemies; nor fear to lose it,] *she attempting to*
160 Thy safety being the motive.   *convince he is*
not trying to
take his daughter
away from
him.

KING LEAR: Out of my sight!

KENT: See better, Lear; and let me still remain
 The true blank of thine eye.   → *stay & let me guide your*
               judgement

KING LEAR: Now, by Apollo,——
       greek god

165 KENT: Now, by Apollo, king,
 Thou swear'st thy gods in vain.

KING LEAR: O, vassal! miscreant!
      [Laying his hand on his sword]

ALBANY: ⎫
     ⎬ Dear sir, forbear.
CORNWALL: ⎭

170 KENT: Do:
 Kill thy physician, and the fee bestow
 Upon thy foul disease. Revoke thy doom;
 Or, whilst I can vent clamour from my throat,
 I'll tell thee thou dost evil.

175 KING LEAR: Hear me, recreant!
 On thine allegiance, hear me!
 Since thou hast sought to make us break our vow,
 Which we durst never yet, and with strain'd pride
 To come between our sentence and our power,
180 Which nor our nature nor our place can bear,
 Our potency made good, take thy reward.
 Five days we do allot thee, for provision ⌐ *king lear gives*
 To shield thee from diseases of the world;   *kent 5 days to*
 And on the sixth to turn thy hated back | *leave and prepare*
185 Upon our kingdom: if, on the tenth day following,|
 Thy banish'd trunk be found in our dominions, ⌐

18

fight your enemies, nor do I fear to lose it, when your safety is at stake.

KING LEAR: *Out of my sight!*

KENT: *See better, Lear, and let me continue to guide your judgment.*

KING LEAR: *Now, by Apollo—*

KENT: *Now, by Apollo, king, you call on the gods in vain.*

KING LEAR: *Oh, you servant! Misbeliever!*
                                          [Starts to draw his sword]

ALBANY, CORNWALL: *Dear sir, control yourself!*

KENT: *Yes, kill your physician and give the fee to the foul disease! Withdraw your proposal, or, while I can still voice my protest, I'll tell you that you're doing wrong.*

KING LEAR: *Hear me, traitor. On your promise of allegiance, hear me. Since you have tried to make me break my vow, which I have never done, and, with excessive pride, tried to come between my decision and my power, which neither my temperament nor my status as king can tolerate, to prove my authority, take your reward. We give you five days to prepare for the troubles of the world. On the sixth day, you will turn your hated back to our kingdom. If, on the tenth day thereafter, your banished body will be found inside our kingdom, it will mean your death. Go away! By Jupiter, this will not be revoked!*

*king banish
Kent for
marrying
daughter

The moment is thy death. Away! by Jupiter,
This shall not be revoked.

KENT: Fare thee well, king: sith thus thou wilt appear,
190   Freedom lives hence, and banishment is here.
        [To Cordelia]
        The gods to their dear shelter take thee, maid,
        That justly think'st, and hast most rightly said!
        [To Regan and Goneril]
        And your large speeches may your deeds approve,
        That good effects may spring from words of love.
195   Thus Kent, O princes, bids you all adieu;
        He'll shape his old course in a country new.   [Exit]

[Flourish. Re-enter Gloucester, with France, Burgundy, and Attendants]

GLOUCESTER: Here's France and Burgundy, my noble lord.

KING LEAR: My lord of Burgundy.
        We first address towards you, who with this king
200   Hath rivall'd for our daughter: what, in the least,
        Will you require in present dower with her,
        Or cease your quest of love?

BURGUNDY: Most royal majesty,
        I crave no more than what your highness offer'd,
205   Nor will you tender less.

the king banishes
his daughters
love out of
fear he will
take her away
from him &
contrives
to
play matchmaker

KING LEAR: Right noble Burgundy,
        When she was dear to us, we did hold her so;
        But now her price is fall'n. Sir, there she stands:
        If aught within that little seeming substance,
210   Or all of it, with our displeasure pieced,
        And nothing more, may fitly like your grace,
        She's there, and she is yours.

sees his daughter as "that little seeming
substance"

20

KENT: *Farewell, king. Since this is how you want it to be, freedom resides somewhere else, while banishment exists here.* [To Cordelia] *The gods may protect you, young woman. You reason correctly and speak the truth.* [To Regan and Goneril] *May your actions live up to your big words, so that good results may come from flattering words of love. I, Kent, dear princes, say goodbye to everyone. I'll continue to live according to my beliefs in a new country.*

[Kent exits. A trumpet sounds. Gloucester enters with France, Burgundy, and Attendants]

GLOUCESTER: *Here are France and Burgundy, my noble lord.*

KING LEAR: *My lord of Burgundy. We will first ask you. You have competed for our daughter's hand with this king. What is the minimum dowry you request so you will continue to court her?*

BURGUNDY: *Most royal king, I demand no more than what you had offered me; you will not offer any less.*

KING LEAR: *Right, noble Burgundy, when she was loved by us, we considered her to be precious. But now her price has decreased. Sir, there she stands. If there is any part of this worthless creature, or all of it, with the addition of my disapproval and nothing more, that will please your Grace, she's right there, and she is yours.*

BURGUNDY: I know no answer.

215 KING LEAR: Will you, with those infirmities she owes,
Unfriended, new-adopted to our hate,
Dower'd with our curse, and stranger'd with our oath,
Take her, or leave her?

BURGUNDY: Pardon me, royal sir;
Election makes not up on such conditions.

220 KING LEAR: Then leave her, sir; for, by the power that made me,
I tell you all her wealth. *[To King of France]*
For you, great king,
I would not from your love make such a stray,
To match you where I hate; therefore beseech you
225 To avert your liking a more worthier way
Than on a wretch whom nature is ashamed
Almost to acknowledge hers.

FRANCE: This is most strange.
That she, that even but now was your best object,
230 The argument of your praise, balm of your age,
Most best, most dearest, should in this trice of time
Commit a thing so monstrous, to dismantle
So many folds of favour. Sure, her offence
Must be of such unnatural degree,
235 That monsters it, or your fore-vouch'd affection
Fall'n into taint: which to believe of her,
Must be a faith that reason without miracle
Could never plant in me.

CORDELIA: I yet beseech your majesty,—
240 If for I want that glib and oily art,
To speak and purpose not; since what I well intend,
I'll do't before I speak,—that you make known
It is no vicious blot, murder, or foulness,
No unchaste action, or dishonour'd step,

(handwritten margin notes:)
her betrayal (or so thought) caused him to believe she is one *whom nature is ashamed almost to acknowledge hers."

France wonders how = his love for her lost over night?

22

BURGUNDY: *I have no answer.*

KING LEAR: *Will you—with the defects she possesses, without a friend, a new object of our hate, cursed, and alienated from us by oath—take her, or leave her?*

BURGUNDY: *Pardon me, royal sir; a decision is impossible under these conditions.*

KING LEAR: *Then leave her, sir, because, on my word, I have described her worth. [To France] As for you, great king, I would not neglect your love by setting you up with someone I hate. Therefore, I beg you to turn your interest toward someone more deserving than a wretch who is despised even by Nature.*

FRANCE: *It is very strange that she, who until now was your most favored object of love, the theme of your praise, the comfort of your old age, the best and dearest, should, in this short moment, have done something so horrible that it would lead to the loss of your love. Surely, her offense must be extremely terrible if it discredits the love you previously declared. Unless a miracle is involved, my reason would never allow me to believe this of her.*

CORDELIA: *I beg your majesty—although I may lack the persuasive and slippery skill to speak without intending to live up to what I say, since what I intend to do, I'll do it before I even say it—to announce that it is no evil plan, murder, immorality, no impure action, or dishonorable deed on my part that has deprived me of your grace and favor, but merely a lack of something I don't*

245 That hath deprived me of your grace and favour;
    But even for want of that for which I am richer,
    A still-soliciting eye, and such a tongue
    As I am glad I have not, though not to have it
    Hath lost me in your liking.

Cordelia tells
sue sees her
greedy
father & is glad
he hates her.

250 KING LEAR: Better thou
    Hadst not been born than not to have pleased me better.

King lear wishes she wasn't born

FRANCE: Is it but this,—a tardiness in nature
    Which often leaves the history unspoke
    That it intends to do? My lord of Burgundy,
255 What say you to the lady? Love's not love
    When it is mingled with regards that stand
    Aloof from the entire point. Will you have her?
    She is herself a dowry.

France
questions loving
her ...
she has so many
unsaid strings
attached.

BURGUNDY: Royal Lear,
260 Give but that portion which yourself proposed,
    And here I take Cordelia by the hand,
    Duchess of Burgundy.

makes an
offer
of
negotiation

KING LEAR: Nothing: I have sworn; I am firm.

265 BURGUNDY: I am sorry, then, you have so lost a father
    That you must lose a husband.

CORDELIA: Peace be with Burgundy!
    Since that respects of fortune are his love,
    I shall not be his wife.

✓ Cordelia values love (kent)

FRANCE: Fairest Cordelia, that art most rich, being poor;
270 Most choice, forsaken; and most loved, despised!
    Thee and thy virtues here I seize upon:
    Be it lawful I take up what's cast away.
    Gods, gods! 'tis strange that from their cold'st neglect
    My love should kindle to inflamed respect.

while Burgundy + king lear are
cold to her he is growing fonder.

24

value anyway: An eye constantly seeking favors and the kind of tongue I am glad I don't have, even though this has cost me your affection.

KING LEAR: It would have been better you hadn't been born than not to have pleased me better!

FRANCE: Is that what it is? A natural hesitation that prevents her from describing the actions she intends to do? My lord of Burgundy, what do you say to this lady? Love is not truly love when it's mixed up with irrelevant considerations. Will you take her? She is in herself a dowry.

BURGUNDY: Royal Lear, give the dowry that you yourself proposed, and I will take Cordelia's hand and make her the Duchess of Burgundy.

KING LEAR: Nothing! I have sworn it, and I am resolute.

BURGUNDY: [To Cordelia] In that case, I am sorry that you have lost a father this way, and must, therefore, lose a husband.

CORDELIA: May peace be with Burgundy. Since considerations of wealth are his idea of love, I will not be his wife.

FRANCE: Fairest Cordelia, who is valuable in her poverty, superior even though she is forsaken, and loved even though she is despised. I claim you and your virtues, if I am allowed to take what has been cast away. Gods, gods! It is strange that out of their cold neglect, my love should grow so passionately. Your

275   Thy dowerless daughter, king, thrown to my chance,
    Is queen of us, of ours, and our fair France:
    Not all the dukes of waterish Burgundy
    Can buy this unprized precious maid of me.
    Bid them farewell, Cordelia, though unkind:
280   Thou losest here, a better where to find.

France believes yes she is losing a place but is gaining something more valueable + better.

KING LEAR: Thou hast her, France: let her be thine; for we
    Have no such daughter, nor shall ever see
    That face of hers again. Therefore be gone
    Without our grace, our love, our benison.
285   Come, noble Burgundy.

King Lear says have her, then we hate you too.

[Flourish. Exeunt all but King of France, Goneril, Regan, and Cordelia]

FRANCE: Bid farewell to your sisters.

CORDELIA: The jewels of our father, with wash'd eyes
    Cordelia leaves you: I know you what you are;
    And like a sister am most loath to call
290   Your faults as they are named. Use well our father:
    To your professed bosoms I commit him
    But yet, alas, stood I within his grace,
    I would prefer him to a better place.
    So, farewell to you both.

Cornelia tells her sisters to show her father love

295 REGAN: Prescribe not us our duties.

sister angry to Cordelia

GONERIL: Let your study
    Be to content your lord, who hath received you
    At fortune's alms. You have obedience scanted,
    And well are worth the want that you have wanted.

sister says you deserve the lack of affection you have given father

300 CORDELIA: Time shall unfold what plaited cunning hides:
    Who cover faults, at last shame them derides.
    Well may you prosper!

dowerless daughter, king, mine through acts of good fortune, is my queen, queen of my possessions, and of beautiful France. Not all the dukes of weak Burgundy can buy this unvalued but precious maid from me. Say goodbye to them, Cordelia, even though they are unkind. You will lose this place, but find a better place elsewhere.

KING LEAR: You can have her, France! She's yours because we have no such daughter, nor will we ever see her face again! Therefore leave—without our affection, our love, and our blessing. Come, noble Burgundy.

[A trumpet sounds. All except for France, Goneril, Regan, and Cordelia exit]

FRANCE: Say goodbye to your sisters.

CORDELIA: Our father's treasures! Cordelia leaves you with tears. I know you for what you are, but, as your sister, I am unwilling to reveal your faults. Treat our father well. I commit him to the love you have professed for him. But, if I were still in his favor, I would restore him to a better position. So farewell to both of you.

REGAN: Do not tell us what our duties are.

GONERIL: Be concerned with pleasing your lord, who has saved you from poverty. You have neglected obedience and deserve to suffer the same lack of affection from your husband that you have shown to your father.

CORDELIA: Time will uncover what is concealed by deceit. Whoever hides faults will eventually be exposed by shame. Good luck to you

ACT I SCENE I

FRANCE: Come, my fair Cordelia.

[Exeunt King of France and Cordelia]

GONERIL: Sister, it is not a little I have to say of what most nearly
305   appertains to us both. I think our father will hence to-night.

REGAN: That's most certain, and with you; next month with us.

GONERIL: You see how full of changes his age is; the observation we
have made of it hath not been little: he always loved our sister
most; and with what poor judgment he hath now cast her off
310   appears too grossly.

REGAN: 'Tis the infirmity of his age: yet he hath ever but slenderly
known himself.

foreshadowment
or
king?
Lear?

GONERIL: The best and soundest of his time hath been but rash; then
315   must we look to receive from his age, not alone the imperfections of long-engraffed condition, but therewithal the unruly
waywardness that infirm and choleric years bring with them.

REGAN: Such unconstant starts are we like to have from him as this
of Kent's banishment.

GONERIL: There is further compliment of leavetaking between France
320   and him. Pray you, let's hit together: if our father carry authority with such dispositions as he bears, this last surrender of his
will but offend us.

foreshadowment
again.

REGAN: We shall further think on 't.

GONERIL: We must do something, and i' the heat.

[Exeunt]

28

FRANCE: *Come, my fair Cordelia.*

[France and Cordelia exit]

GONERIL: *Sister, there is a lot I have to say about what concerns us both. I think our father will leave tonight.*

REGAN: *That's for sure, and he will go with you; next month, he will stay with us.*

GONERIL: *You see how he has changed with age; we have noticed it many times. He always loved our sister most. The way he has now banished her shows his poor judgment.*

REGAN: *It's the frailty of his old age. Yet, he has never had full control over himself.*

GONERIL: *Even throughout his best years, he was always impetuous. So now, in his old age, we must not only expect to deal with his deeply-rooted imperfections, but, along with that, with the willfulness that comes with weak and angry old age.*

REGAN: *We're likely to encounter more rash actions such as Kent's banishment.*

GONERIL: *There are further departure formalities between France and him. Please, let's work together in our course of action. If our father continues to assert his authority with the temper he has displayed, his recent surrender of his kingdom to us will turn out to do us harm.*

REGAN: *We'll think about it some more.*

GONERIL: *We must strike while the iron is hot.*

[They exit]

SCENE II

The Earl of Gloucester's castle.

[Enter Edmund, with a letter]

EDMUND: Thou, nature, art my goddess; to thy law
    My services are bound. Wherefore should I
    Stand in the plague of custom, and permit
    The curiosity of nations to deprive me,
5   For that I am some twelve or fourteen moon-shines
    Lag of a brother? Why bastard? wherefore base?
    When my dimensions are as well compact,
    My mind as generous, and my shape as true,
    As honest madam's issue? Why brand they us
10   With base? with baseness? bastardy? base, base?
    Who, in the lusty stealth of nature, take
    More composition and fierce quality
    Than doth, within a dull, stale, tired bed,
    Go to the creating a whole tribe of fops,
15   Got 'tween asleep and wake? Well, then,
    Legitimate Edgar, I must have your land:
    Our father's love is to the bastard Edmund
    As to the legitimate: fine word,–legitimate!
    Well, my legitimate, if this letter speed,
20   And my invention thrive, Edmund the base
    Shall top the legitimate. I grow; I prosper:
    Now, gods, stand up for bastards!

[Enter Gloucester]

GLOUCESTER: Kent banish'd thus! and France in choler parted!
    And the king gone to-night! subscribed his power!
25   Confined to exhibition! All this done
    Upon the gad! Edmund, how now! what news?

EDMUND: So please your lordship, none.   *[Putting up the letter]*

30

SCENE II

The Earl of Gloucester's castle.

[Edmund enters, with a letter]

EDMUND: *You are my goddess, nature. My services are at your command. Why should I remain subject to customary conventions and allow the narrow-mindedness of society to deprive me of my rights? Because I am twelve or fourteen months younger than my brother? Why am I a bastard? Why inferior? My bodily parts are as well-proportioned, my mind as dynamic, and my appearance as true to my father's likeness as the chaste woman's son. Why do they mark us with inferiority, with unworthiness? Why a bastard? Why inferior, inferior? We received a better constitution and a more vigorous strength through the enjoyment of a healthy sexual appetite than did a whole tribe of fools who were conceived at night in a dull and boring marriage bed. Well then, legitimate Edgar, I must have your land! Our father loves the bastard son Edmund as much as the legitimate son Edgar. As to the legitimate: fine word, "legitimate". Well, my legitimate, if this letter is a success and my plan goes well, Edmund, the inferior, will surpass the legitimate son. I'll progress, I'll prosper! Well then, gods, stand up for bastards!*

[Gloucester enters]

GLOUCESTER: *Kent is banished. And king of France departed in anger. And the king left tonight. Limited his power. Is restricted to an allowance of money. All of this happened in the spur of the moment. Edmund, how are you? Do you have any news?*

EDMUND: *If it pleases your lordship, none.* [He slowly hides his letter]

GLOUCESTER: Why so earnestly seek you to put up that letter?

EDMUND: I know no news, my lord.

— Edmund lying about letter

30   GLOUCESTER: What paper were you reading?

EDMUND: Nothing, my lord.

GLOUCESTER: No? What needed, then, that terrible dispatch of it into
your pocket? the quality of nothing hath not such need to hide
itself. Let's see: come, if it be nothing, I shall not need
35   spectacles.

why can I not see it it is nothing?

EDMUND: I beseech you, sir, pardon me: it is a letter from my
brother, that I have not all o'er-read; and for so much as I have
erused, I find it not fit for your o'er-looking.

— Edmund received the letter from his brother.

GLOUCESTER: Give me the letter, sir.

40   EDMUND: I shall offend, either to detain or give it. The contents, as
in part I understand them, are to blame.

letter is unpleasant

GLOUCESTER: Let's see, let's see.

EDMUND: I hope, for my brother's justification, he wrote this but as
an essay or taste of my virtue.

45   GLOUCESTER: [Reads]
'This policy and reverence of age makes the world bitter to the best
of our times; keeps our fortunes from us till our oldness cannot rel-
ish them. I begin to find an idle and fond bondage in the oppression
of aged tyranny; who sways, not as it hath power, but as it is suffered.
50   Come to me, that of this I may speak more. If our father would sleep
till I waked him, you should half his revenue for ever, and live the
beloved of your brother,
                                                Edgar.'

Edgar, ~~Gloucester~~ Edmund's brother is complaining of old part the potential they could have had without it

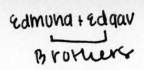
Edmund + Edgar
Brothers

GLOUCESTER: *Why are you trying so hard to hide that letter?*

EDMUND: *I have no news, my lord.*

GLOUCESTER: *What is the document you were you reading?*

EDMUND: *Nothing, my lord.*

GLOUCESTER: *No? Why did you stash it so quickly in your- pocket? If it was nothing, you wouldn't have to hide it. Let's see. Come, if it's nothing, I won't need spectacles.*

EDMUND: *I beg you, sir, forgive me. It's a letter from my brother that I have not finished reading. Judging from the parts I have read carefully, I believe it's not suitable for your inspection.*

GLOUCESTER: *Give me the letter, sir!*

EDMUND: *I'll offend you whether I keep it or give it to you. The contents, as I understand them so far, are unpleasant.*

GLOUCESTER: *Let's see, let's see!*

EDMUND: *I hope, for my brother's sake, that he only wrote this as a trial or test of my virtue.*

GLOUCESTER: [Reads]
"This policy of respecting old people makes the world unpleasant throughout the best years of our lives. It keeps our inheritance from us until we are too old to enjoy it. I begin to understand that oppression by old tyrants is useless and foolish. They don't rule through power, but because we put up with them. Come see me, and I will talk more detailed about this. If our father were dead, you could enjoy half of his income forever and be loved by your brother, Edgar."

Hum–conspiracy!– "Sleep till I waked him,–you should enjoy half his revenue,"–My son Edgar! Had he a hand to write this? a heart and brain to breed it in?–When came this to you? who brought it?

Gloucester wonders how Edmund could believe this.

55

EDMUND: It was not brought me, my lord; there's the cunning of it; I found it thrown in at the casement of my closet.

GLOUCESTER: You know the character to be your brother's?

60 EDMUND: If the matter were good, my lord, I durst swear it were his; but, in respect of that, I would fain think it were not.

GLOUCESTER: It is his.

suspicion of letter actually being from edgar. ?

EDMUND: It is his hand, my lord; but I hope his heart is not in the contents.

Both hope edgar doesn't feel this way.

65 GLOUCESTER: Hath he never heretofore sounded you in this business?

has he ever tried to get your opinion on this?

EDMUND: Never, my lord: but I have heard him oft maintain it to be fit, that, sons at perfect age, and fathers declining, the father should be as ward to the son, and the son manage his revenue.

Edgar has felt this way on old tyranny for our own

70 GLOUCESTER: O villain, villain! His very opinion in the letter! Abhorred villain! Unnatural, detested, brutish villain! worse than brutish! Go, sirrah, seek him; I'll apprehend him: abominable villain! Where is he?

EDMUND: I do not well know, my lord. If it shall please you to suspend your indignation against my brother till you can derive

Hah! Conspiracy? *"If our father were dead, you could enjoy half his income."* My son Edgar? Did he write this? Did he have the heart and brain to come up with this? When did you get this? Who brought it?

EDMUND: It wasn't brought to me, my lord. That's the clever part. I found it thrown through the window of my bedroom.

GLOUCESTER: Do you recognize the handwriting as that of your brother?

EDMUND: If the contents were positive, I would swear it's his. But, with regard to this matter, I'd rather think it's not.

GLOUCESTER: It is his.

EDMUND: It's his handwriting, my lord, but I hope his heart isn't in it.

GLOUCESTER: Has he ever before tried to get your opinion on this subject?

EDMUND: Never, my lord, but I have often heard him argue that, when sons reach maturity and fathers get old, the fathers should give themselves into the care of the sons, and the sons should take over the management of the fathers' affairs.

GLOUCESTER: Oh, the villain, villain! His opinion is stated in the letter. Repulsive villain! Unnatural, detestable, brutish villain. Worse than brutish. Go, son, find him! I'll arrest him, the abominable villain! Where is he?

EDMUND: I am not sure, my lord. If you contain your resentment against my brother until you can gather better evidence that proves his

75   from him better testimony of his intent, you shall run a certain
      course; where, if you violently proceed against him, mistaking
      his purpose, it would make a great gap in your own honour,
      and shake in pieces the heart of his obedience. I dare pawn
      down my life for him, that he hath wrote this to feel my affec-
80   tion to your honour, and to no further pretence of danger.

→ Edmund is slowing down Gloucester

GLOUCESTER: Think you so?

EDMUND: If your honour judge it meet, I will place you where you
      shall hear us confer of this, and by an auricular assurance have
      your satisfaction; and that without any further delay than this
85   very evening.

GLOUCESTER: He cannot be such a monster——

EDMUND: Nor is not, sure.

GLOUCESTER: To his father, that so tenderly and entirely loves him.
      Heaven and earth! Edmund, seek him out: wind me into him,
90   I pray you: frame the business after your own wisdom. I would
      unstate myself, to be in a due resolution.

EDMUND: I will seek him, sir, presently: convey the business as I
      shall find means and acquaint you withal.

95   GLOUCESTER: These late eclipses in the sun and moon portend
      no good to us: though the wisdom of nature can reason it thus
      and thus, yet nature finds itself scourged by the sequent effects:

they all turn to Greek mythology + astrological tendencies

      [love cools, friendship falls off, brothers divide: in cities, muti-
      nies; in countries, discord; in palaces, treason; and the bond
100   cracked 'twixt son and father] This villain of mine comes under
      the prediction; there's son against father: the king falls from bias
      of nature; there's father against child. We have seen the best of
      our time: machinations, hollowness, treachery, and all ruinous
      disorders, follow us disquietly to our graves. Find out this vil-

foreshadowment in [ ]

intentions, you will pursue a safe course of action. But, if you react violently against him and misunderstand his intentions, it will threaten your honor and destroy his loyalty to you. I swear by my life that he has written this in order to test my dedication to your honor and without dangerous intentions.

GLOUCESTER: *Do you think so?*

EDMUND: *If you find it appropriate, I will take you to a place where you can hear us discuss this, and, by hearing it yourself, you can remove your doubts. This can happen no later than tonight.*

GLOUCESTER: *He cannot be such a monster.*

EDMUND: *I'm sure he's not.*

GLOUCESTER: *To his father, who loves him so tenderly and entirely. Heaven and earth! Edmund, find him! Gain his confidence, I beg you. Set up a situation according to your own discretion. I would give anything to have my doubts removed.*

EDMUND: *I will find him at once, sir, manage the business as I see fit, and inform you about everything.*

GLOUCESTER: *These recent eclipses of the sun and the moon foreshadow nothing good for us. Although science can explain the occurrences of eclipses, the world is plagued by the consequences that follow Love cools, friendships break, brothers fight. In cities, there are riots, in countries, there is conflict, in palaces, there is treason, and the bonds between father and son fall apart. This villain comes as predicted: There's son against father. The king acts contrary to his natural tendencies: There's father against child. We have seen great things in our time: Plots, deception, treachery,*

105 lain, Edmund; it shall lose thee nothing; do it carefully. And the
noble and true-hearted Kent banished! his
offence, honesty! 'Tis strange.   *[Exit]*

EDMUND: This is the excellent foppery of the world, that, when we
are sick in fortune—often the surfeit of our own behavior,—we
110 make guilty of our disasters the sun, the moon, and the stars: as
if we were villains by necessity; fools by heavenly compulsion;
knaves, thieves, and treachers, by spherical predominance;
drunkards, liars, and adulterers, by an enforced obedience of
planetary influence; and all that we are evil in, by a divine
115 thrusting on: an admirable evasion of whoremaster man, to lay
his goatish disposition to the charge of a star! My father com-
pounded with my mother under the dragon's tail; and my nativ-
ity was under Ursa major; so that it follows, I am rough and
lecherous. Tut, I should have been that I am, had the maidenli-
120 est star in the firmament twinkled on my bastardizing. Edgar—

*Edmund reeutes belief in astrologu having toao
w/ scenario outcomes. He believes it is a mans
aoing to be evil or good.*

[Enter Edgar]
And pat he comes like the catastrophe of the old comedy: my
cue is villanous melancholy, with a sigh like Tom o' Bedlam. O,
these eclipses do portend these divisions! fa, sol, la, mi.

125 EDGAR: How now, brother Edmund! what serious contemplation are
you in?

EDMUND: I am thinking, brother, of a prediction I read this other
day, what should follow these eclipses.

EDGAR: Do you busy yourself about that?

38

and disastrous disorder follow us sadly to our graves. Uncover this villain, Edmund. You will lose nothing by it. Do it carefully. And the noble and loyal Kent is banished! His offense: honesty. It is strange!

[Gloucester exits]

EDMUND: This is the absolute stupidity of this world! When we have bad luck, often as a result of our own excessive behavior, we hold the sun, the moon, and the stars responsible for our misery. As if we were villains without a choice, fools of heavenly predestination, knaves, thieves, and traitors due to the constellation of the stars, drunkards, liars, and adulterers because of the influence of the planets. As if all evil acts were caused by divine force! An admirable excuse for a lecherous man, to blame his shameful acts on the stars. My father lay with my mother under a descending moon, and I was born under the great bear. So that's why I am rough and lustful. Pah! I would have turned out the way I am even if the most chaste star in the firmament had twinkled over my illegitimate conception. Edgar—

[Edgar enters]
And here he comes, like the resolution at the end of an old-fashioned comedy. My look displays evil melancholy, with a sigh like that of a mad beggar. Oh, these eclipses do foretell conflict! Fa, so, la, mi. [He hums several notes]

EDGAR: How are you, brother Edmund? What are you contemplating so seriously?

EDMUND: My brother, I am thinking about a prediction I read the other day about the consequences of these eclipses.

EDGAR: Are you concerned with things like that?

EDMUND: I promise you, the effects he writes of succeed unhappily;
130   as of unnaturalness between the child and the parent; death,
    dearth, dissolutions of ancient amities; divisions in state, men-
    aces and maledictions against king and nobles; needless dif-
    fidences, banishment of friends, dissipation of cohorts, nuptial
    breaches, and I know not what.

Hinting through astrology a message about letters.

135 EDGAR: How long have you been a sectary astronomical?

EDMUND: Come, come; when saw you my father last?

EDGAR: Why, the night gone by.

EDMUND: Spake you with him?

EDGAR: Ay, two hours together.

140 EDMUND: Parted you in good terms? Found you no displeasure in
    him by word or countenance?

EDGAR: None at all.   → *was Edgar lying in the letter?*
    Did he write the letter?

EDMUND: Bethink yourself wherein you may have offended him: and
    at my entreaty forbear his presence till some little time hath
145   qualified the heat of his displeasure; which at this instant so
    rageth in him, that with the mischief of your person it would
    scarcely allay.

EDGAR: Some villain hath done me wrong.

EDMUND: That's my fear. I pray you, have a continent forbearance
150   till the spied of his rage goes slower; and, as I say, retire with
    me to my lodging, from whence I will fitly bring you to hear my
    lord speak: pray ye, go; there's my key: if you do stir abroad, go
    armed.

Edmund advises Edgar to
stay away from their father
+ his rage.

EDMUND: I promise you, the consequences I read about are unpleasant: the lack of affection between a child and a father; death, famine, and the termination of old friendships; disagreements in countries, threats and curses against kings and noblemen; groundless suspicions, the banishment of friends, desertion of troops, marital conflict , and I don't know what else.

EDGAR: How long have you been a devotee of astrology?

EDMUND: Come on, come on; when did you last see my father?

EDGAR: Well, last night.

EDMUND: Did you speak with him?

EDGAR: Yes, for two hours.

EDMUND: Did you part on good terms? Did you sense any displeasure in his words or demeanor?

EDGAR: None at all.

EDMUND: Try to remember how you may have offended him. I advise you to avoid his presence until some time has passed and his displeasure has calmed down. Right now, he is so angry that any physical injury to you would not even make him feel better.

EDGAR: Some villain has done me wrong.

EDMUND: That's what I'm afraid of. I advise you to stay well out of his way, until he calms down, and, as I say, come home with me, where I'll let you hear what my lord says at a suitable time. Now, go. Here's my key. If you do go out, go armed.

EDGAR: Armed, brother!

155 EDMUND: Brother, I advise you to the best; go armed: I am no honest
man if there be any good meaning towards you: I have told you
what I have seen and heard; but faintly, nothing like the image
and horror of it: pray you, away.

EDGAR: Shall I hear from you anon?

160 EDMUND: I do serve you in this business.   [Exit Edgar]
A credulous father! and a brother noble,
Whose nature is so far from doing harms,
That he suspects none: on whose foolish honesty
My practises ride easy! I see the business.
165 Let me, if not by birth, have lands by wit:
All with me's meet that I can fashion fit.   [Exit]

Both Lear + Gloucester have loyal children — truly loyal: Edgar + Cordelia as well as ill-intention children: Goneril, Reagan, Edmund.

SCENE III

Fathers have a blindness to the truth.

The Duke of Albany's palace.

[Enter Goneril, and Oswald, her steward]

GONERIL: Did my father strike my gentleman for chiding of his fool?

OSWALD: Yes, madam.

GONERIL: By day and night he wrongs me; every hour
He flashes into one gross crime or other,
5   That sets us all at odds: I'll not endure it:
His knights grow riotous, and himself upbraids us
On every trifle. When he returns from hunting,

42

Gloucaster seems
to have a preexisting
eear his children will destroy him ⟶ believes Edmund now
ACT I SCENE III *away.*

EDGAR: Armed, brother?

EDMUND: Brother, I give you my best advice: Arm yourself! I wouldn't be honest if I said there were any good intentions toward you. I have told you what I have seen and heard, though barely the horrible reality of it. Go away now.

EDGAR: Will I hear from you soon?

EDMUND: I'll help you with this matter.

[Edgar exits]
A naïve father and a noble brother, who is so incapable of mischief that he never expects someone could do it to him. His foolish honesty cannot stand against my intrigues. I see what I ho e to do: If I cannot have property due to my illegitimate birth, I'll r   by using my wit. Everything is fine by me that works in my fav

SCENE III

The Duke of Albany's palace.

[Goneril and Oswald, her steward, enter]

GONERIL: Did my father strike my gentleman attendant for scolding his fool?

OSWALD: Yes, madam.

GONERIL: He does me wrong all the time. Every hour he commits one awful offense or another that causes conflict among all of us. I will not tolerate it. His knights act disorderly, and he reproaches us for every little thing. When he returns from hunting, I won't speak with him. Tell him I'm sick. If you fall short

43

I will not speak with him; say I am sick:
If you come slack of former services,
10   You shall do well; the fault of it I'll answer.

OSWALD: He's coming, madam; I hear him.   *[Horns within]*

GONERIL: Put on what weary negligence you please,
You and your fellows; I'll have it come to question:
If he dislike it, let him to our sister,
15   Whose mind and mine, I know, in that are one,
Not to be over-ruled. Idle old man,
That still would manage those authorities
That he hath given away! Now, by my life,
Old fools are babes again; and must be used
20   With cheques as flatteries,—when they are seen abused.
Remember what I tell you.

Goneril e edmund have similar outlooks on despising the elderly.

OSWALD: Well, madam.

GONERIL: And let his knights have colder looks among you;
What grows of it, no matter; advise your fellows so:
25   I would breed from hence occasions, and I shall,
That I may speak: I'll write straight to my sister,
To hold my very course. Prepare for dinner.   *[Exeunt]*

• Goneril is taking on power + acting on dismaying her father.

44

of your former services to him, that will be all right. I'll take responsibility for it.

OSWALD: *He's coming, madam. I hear him.*

[Hunting horns sound]

GONERIL: *You and your fellow servants can neglect his wishes. I want to provoke him into a confrontation. If he's displeased with it, let him go to my sister. Her opinion and mine, I know, are the same, and we will not be ruled by him. Foolish old man, who still wants to claim the authority he has given away. Now, I swear, senile fools become babies again, and must be controlled and not flattered when they are obviously misguided. Remember what I tell you.*

OSWALD: *Yes, I will, madam.*

GONERIL: *And let his knights receive cold looks from you, no matter what the consequences may be. Tell this to your fellow servants as well. From now on, I will create opportunities that allow me to speak my mind. I will immediately write to my sister and tell her to do the same. Prepare for dinner.*

[They exit]

SCENE IV

A hall in the same.

[Enter Kent, disguised]

KENT: If but as well I other accents borrow,
    That can my speech defuse, my good intent
    May carry through itself to that full issue
    For which I razed my likeness. Now, banish'd Kent,
5   If thou canst serve where thou dost stand condemn'd,
    So may it come, thy master, whom thou lovest,
    Shall find thee full of labours.

[Horns within. Enter King Lear, Knights, and Attendants]

KING LEAR: Let me not stay a jot for dinner; go get it ready.
                                    [Exit an Attendant]
    How now! what art thou?

10   KENT: A man, sir.

KING LEAR: What dost thou profess? what wouldst thou with us?

KENT: I do profess to be no less than I seem; to serve him truly that
    will put me in trust: to love him that is honest; to converse with
    him that is wise, and says little; to fear judgment; to fight when
15   I cannot choose; and to eat no fish.

KING LEAR: What art thou?

KENT: A very honest-hearted fellow, and as poor as the king.

KING LEAR: If thou be as poor for a subject as he is for a king, thou
    art poor enough. What wouldst thou?

46

SCENE IV

A hall in the same.

[Kent enters in disguise]

KENT: *If I could add another accent to my disguise, to change my voice, my good intentions may lead to the perfect outcome for which I erased my former appearance. Now, banished Kent, if you can serve where you were condemned, it may happen that your master, whom you love, will consider you a great servant.*

[Horns sound. Lear, Knights, and Attendants enter]

KING LEAR: *Don't let me wait for dinner. Go get it ready.*
                                    [An Attendant exits]
    What now? What are you?

KENT: *A man, sir.*

KING LEAR: *What skill do you have? What is your business here?*

KENT: *I claim to be no less than what I seem to be, to serve any man faithfully who gives me his confidence, to love the man who is honorable, to associate with the man who is wise and speaks few words, to fear God's judgment, to fight when I have no choice, and to follow the rules.*

KING LEAR: *What are you?*

KENT: *A very sincere man who is as poor as the king is.*

KING LEAR: *If you are as poor a subject as he is a king, you are quite poor. What do you want?*

20 KENT: Service.

KING LEAR: Who wouldst thou serve?

KENT: You.

KING LEAR: Dost thou know me, fellow?

KENT: No, sir; but you have that in your countenance which I would
25   fain call master.

KING LEAR: What's that?

KENT: Authority.

KING LEAR: What services canst thou do?

KENT: I can keep honest counsel, ride, run, mar a curious tale in
30   telling it, and deliver a plain message bluntly: that which ordi-
    nary men are fit for, I am qualified in; and the best of me is dili-
    gence.

KING LEAR: How old art thou?

KENT: Not so young, sir, to love a woman for singing, nor so old to
35   dote on her for any thing: I have years on my back forty eight.

I have years on my back seventeen

KING LEAR: Follow me; thou shalt serve me: if I like thee no worse
    after dinner, I will not part from thee yet. Dinner, ho, dinner!
    Where's my knave? my fool? Go you, and call my fool hither.
                    [Exit an Attendant]

[Enter Oswald]
    You, you, sirrah, where's my daughter?

KENT: *Employment.*

KING LEAR: *Whom do you want to work for?*

KENT: *You.*

KING LEAR: *Do you know me, fellow?*

KENT: *No, sir, but something in your appearance demands respect.*

KING LEAR: *What's that?*

KENT: *Authority.*

KING LEAR: *What services can you perform?*

KENT: *I can keep confidential matters secret, ride, run, and spoil a complicated story by telling it. I am qualified for anything an ordinary man can do; diligence is my best quality.*

KING LEAR: *How old are you?*

KENT: *Not young enough to love a woman for singing, not old enough to dote on her for anything else. I am forty-eight years old.*

KING LEAR: *Follow me; you will be my servant. If I don't like you any less after dinner, I won't dismiss you. Dinner, quick, dinner! Where is my servant boy,; where is my fool?* [To an Attendant]
Go and bring my fool here. [An Attendant exits]

[Oswald enters]
You, you fellow. Where's my daughter?

40   OSWALD: So please you,—   [Exit]

KING LEAR: What says the fellow there? Call the clotpoll back.
                                     [Exit a Knight]
  Where's my fool, ho? I think the world's asleep.

[Re-enter Knight]
  How now! where's that mongrel?

KNIGHT: He says, my lord, your daughter is not well.

45   KING LEAR: Why came not the slave back to me when I called him.

KNIGHT: Sir, he answered me in the roundest manner, he would
  not.

KING LEAR: He would not!

KNIGHT: My lord, I know not what the matter is; but, to my judg-
50   ment, your highness is not entertained with that ceremonious
  affection as you were wont; there's a great abatement of kindness appears as well in the general dependants as in the duke
  himself also and your daughter.

KING LEAR: Ha! sayest thou so?

55   KNIGHT: I beseech you, pardon me, my lord, if I be mistaken; for my
  duty cannot be silent when I think your highness wronged.

KING LEAR: Thou but rememberest me of mine own conception: I
  have perceived a most faint neglect of late; which I have rather
  blamed as mine own jealous curiosity than as a very pretence
  and purpose of unkindness: I will look further into 't. But
60   here's my fool? I have not seen him this two days.

50

OSWALD: Excuse me—   [He exits]

KING LEAR: What did that fellow say? Call the blockhead back!
                                                    [A knight exits]
   Where's my fool? I think the world's asleep.

[Knight reenters]
   Well then, where is that man?

KNIGHT: He says, my lord, that your daughter is not well.

KING LEAR: Why didn't the slave come back to me when I called him?

KNIGHT: Sir, he answered me plainly that he would not come back.

KING LEAR: He would not.

KNIGHT: My lord, I don't know what is going on, but I have the impression
   that your highness is not treated with the respect that you're used to
   receiving as a father and a king. There's a lack of affection in all the
   servants, as well as the by duke himself and your daughter.

KING LEAR: Ha! Is that what you say?

KNIGHT: I beg you to forgive me, my lord, if I am wrong, but it is my duty
   to speak when I believe your highness is being wronged.

KING LEAR: You only remind me of the impression I've had myself. I have
   noticed a lazy neglect lately, which I have blamed more on my own
   jealous sensitivity than on a deliberate display of unfriendliness. I
   will look into it further. But where's my fool? I haven't seen him in
   two days.

KNIGHT: Since my young lady's going into France, sir, the fool hath
much pined away.

KING LEAR: No more of that; I have noted it well. Go you, and tell
65   my daughter I would speak with her.   *[Exit an Attendant]*
Go you, call hither my fool.   *[Exit an Attendant]*

[Re-enter Oswald]
O, you sir, you, come you hither, sir: who am I, sir?

OSWALD: My lady's father.

KING LEAR: 'My lady's father'! my lord's knave: your whoreson dog!
70   you slave! you cur!

OSWALD: I am none of these, my lord; I beseech your pardon.

KING LEAR: Do you bandy looks with me, you rascal?
    [Striking him]

OSWALD: I'll not be struck, my lord.

KENT: Nor tripped neither, you base football player.
    [Tripping up his heels]

75 KING LEAR: I thank thee, fellow; thou servest me, and I'll love thee.

KENT: Come, sir, arise, away! I'll teach you differences: away, away!
if you will measure your lubber's length again, tarry: but away!
go to; have you wisdom? so.   *[Pushes Oswald out]*

KING LEAR: Now, my friendly knave, I thank thee: there's earnest of
80   thy service.   *[Giving Kent money]*

- king lear resorts to
anger & violence asap (70 — 75)
when his control & power is in any
way questioned.

KNIGHT: *Since my young lady [Cordelia] has gone to France, he has been very upset.*

KING LEAR: *No more of that! I have noticed it myself. You go and tell my daughter I want to speak with her.*
[An attendant exits]

You, go and bring my fool here.

[An Attendant exits. Oswald reenters]
Oh, you, sir, come here, sir. Who am I, sir?

OSWALD: *My lady's father.*

KING LEAR: *"My lady's father." My lord's servant. You lousy dog! You slave! You cur!*

OSWALD: *I am none of that, my lord, I beg your pardon.*

KING LEAR: *Are you talking back to me, you rascal?*
[He strikes Oswald]

OSWALD: *I won't be struck, my lord!*

KENT: *Or tripped either, you worthless brute!* [He trips him]

KING LEAR: *I thank you, fellow. You serve me, and I will treat you well.*

KENT: *Come, sir, get up and leave. I'll put you in your place. Go away, away. Don't you have any common sense?*
[He pushes Oswald out]

KING LEAR: *Now, my friend, I thank you. Here's an advance payment for your services.* [He gives Kent money]

[Enter Fool]

FOOL: Let me hire him too: here's my coxcomb.

[Offering Kent his cap]

KING LEAR: How now, my pretty knave! how dost thou?

FOOL: Sirrah, you were best take my coxcomb.

KENT: Why, fool?

85 FOOL: Why, for taking one's part that's out of favour: nay, an thou
canst not smile as the wind sits, thou'lt catch cold shortly:
there, take my coxcomb: why, this fellow has banished two on's
daughters, and did the third a blessing against his will; if thou
follow him, thou must needs wear my coxcomb. How now,
90 nuncle! Would I had two coxcombs and two daughters!

disagreement *(handwritten in margin)*

KING LEAR: Why, my boy?

FOOL: If I gave them all my living, I'd keep my coxcombs myself.
There's mine; beg another of thy daughters.

KING LEAR: Take heed, sirrah; the whip.

anger *(handwritten)*

95 FOOL: Truth's a dog must to kennel; he must be whipped out, when
Lady the brach may stand by the fire and stink.

KING LEAR: A pestilent gall to me!

anger. *(handwritten)*

FOOL: Sirrah, I'll teach thee a speech.

KING LEAR: Do.

(handwritten in left margin, sideways): Anytime king lear re either told no or told something impending loss of control

[Fool enters]

FOOL: Let me hire him, too. Here is my fool's cap.

[He offers Kent his cap]

KING LEAR: Hello there, my boy. How are you?

FOOL: Sir, you'd better take my cap.

KENT: Why, Fool?

FOOL: Why, for taking the side of someone who's out of favor. If you don't side with those in power, you will feel the consequences soon. Here, take my cap. Well, this fellow here has banished two of his daughters and blessed the third one against his will. If you follow him, you must wear my fool's cap. How are you, my uncle? I wish I had two caps and two daughters.

KING LEAR: Why, my boy?

FOOL: If I gave them all I own, I'd be twice the fool. Here's my cap. Get another one from your daughters.

KING LEAR: Be careful, sir, or I'll get the whip!

FOOL: Truth is like a dog that is sent to the kennel, while Falsehood can stand by the fire and stink.

KING LEAR: This irritates me.

FOOL: Sir, I'll teach you something.

KING LEAR: Please do.

100   FOOL: Mark it, nuncle:

> Have more than thou showest,
> Speak less than thou knowest,
> Lend less than thou owest,
> Ride more than thou goest,
105 > Learn more than thou trowest,
> Set less than thou throwest;
> Leave thy drink and thy whore,
> And keep in-a-door,
> And thou shalt have more
> Than two tens to a score.

[handwritten margin note: Fool tells king lear to be humble & mysterious to gain true profit.]

KENT: This is nothing, fool.

FOOL: Then 'tis like the breath of an unfee'd lawyer; you gave me
nothing for't. Can you make no use of nothing, nuncle?

KING LEAR: Why, no, boy; nothing can be made out of nothing.

115   FOOL: *[To Kent]* Prithee, tell him, so much the rent of his land
comes to: he will not believe a fool.

KING LEAR: A bitter fool!

FOOL: Dost thou know the difference, my boy, between a bitter fool
and a sweet fool?

120   KING LEAR: No, lad; teach me.

FOOL:

> That lord that counsell'd thee
> To give away thy land,
> Come place him here by me,
> Do thou for him stand:
125 > The sweet and bitter fool
> Will presently appear;
> The one in motley here,
> The other found out there.

56

FOOL: *Remember this, my uncle:*
> *Have more than you show, speak less than you know,*
> *lend less than you possess, ride more than you walk,*
> *learn more than you believe, gamble less than you can*
> *afford, give up drinking and whores, stay inside, and*
> *you will save money and gain a profit.*

KENT: *This is nothing, Fool!*

FOOL: *Then it's like the advice of a lawyer who doesn't get paid. I got nothing for it. Can't you make use of nothing, uncle?*

KING LEAR: *Well, no boy; nothing can be made out of nothing.*

FOOL: *[To Kent] Will you tell him that that's what his income is? He won't believe a fool.*

KING LEAR: *A bitter fool!*

FOOL: *Do you know the difference, my boy, between a bitter fool and a sweet fool?*

KING LEAR: *No boy, teach me.*

FOOL:
> *That lord who advised you to give away your land,*
> *bring him here to me. You stand in for him. The*
> *sweet and the bitter fool will appear at once. The one*
> *dressed as I am here, the other one [the bitter one]*
> *right there [He points at Lear].*

KING LEAR: Dost thou call me fool, boy?

130 FOOL: All thy other titles thou hast given away; that thou wast born with.

KENT: This is not altogether fool, my lord.

FOOL: No, faith, lords and great men will not let me; if I had a monopoly out, they would have part on't: and ladies too, they
135 will not let me have all fool to myself; they'll be snatching. Give me an egg, nuncle, and I'll give thee two crowns.

KING LEAR: What two crowns shall they be?

FOOL: Why, after I have cut the egg in the middle, and eat up the meat, the two crowns of the egg. When thou clovest thy crown
140 i' the middle, and gavest away both parts, thou borest thy ass on thy back o'er the dirt: thou hadst little wit in thy bald crown, when thou gavest thy golden one away. If I speak like myself in this, let him be whipped that first finds it so.

[Singing]   Fools had ne'er less wit in a year;
145   For wise men are grown foppish,
             They know not how their wits to wear,
              Their manners are so apish.

KING LEAR: When were you wont to be so full of songs, sirrah?

FOOL: I have used it, nuncle, ever since thou madest thy daughters
150 thy mothers: for when thou gavest them the rod, and put'st down thine own breeches,

[Singing]   Then they for sudden joy did weep,
              And I for sorrow sung,
             That such a king should play bo-peep,
155   And go the fools among.

KING LEAR: *Are you calling me a fool, boy?*

FOOL: *You have given away all your other titles, but you were born with this one.*

KENT: *He's not entirely a fool, my lord.*

FOOL: *No, truly, lords and great men will not let me be. If I had a monopoly on being a fool, they would want their share. The ladies, too! They would not let me monopolize foolishness. They'd be snatching it away. Give me an egg, uncle, and I'll give you two crowns.*

KING LEAR: *What two crowns would that be?*

FOOL: *Well, after I cut the egg in the middle and eat it, the two remaining eggshells! When you divided your crown and gave away both parts of your kingdom, you wanted to please everyone, but couldn't. You had little wit in your bald crown when you gave the golden one away. If I speak like a fool, whip the one who first finds out that this is true.*

> [Singing] *Fools were never less in demand, because wise men have become foolish and have taken their place, but they don't know how to show their wits, so they act so foolishly.*

KING LEAR: *Since when have you been so full of songs, sir?*

FOOL: *I started singing ever since you turned your daughters into your mother, when you gave them a cane and pulled down your pants.*

> [Singing] *Then they cried out of joy and I sang s᷄ because such a king played a children's ᷄ joined the fools.*

Prithee, nuncle, keep a schoolmaster that can teach thy fool to
lie: I would fain learn to lie.

KING LEAR: An you lie, sirrah, we'll have you whipped.

160 FOOL: I marvel what kin thou and thy daughters are: they'll have me
whipped for speaking true, thou'lt have me whipped for lying;
and sometimes I am whipped for holding my peace. I had rather
be any kind o' thing than a fool: and yet I would not be thee,
nuncle; thou hast pared thy wit o' both sides, and left nothing i'
the middle: here comes one o' the parings.

[Enter Goneril]

165 KING LEAR: How now, daughter! what makes that frontlet on?
Methinks you are too much of late i' the frown.

FOOL: Thou wast a pretty fellow when thou hadst no need to care
for her frowning; now thou art an O without a figure: I am
better than thou art now; I am a fool, thou art nothing. *[To
170 Goneril]* Yes, forsooth, I will hold my tongue; so your face bids
me, though you say nothing.
      Mum, mum,
      He that keeps nor crust nor crum,
      Weary of all, shall want some.
175 *[Pointing to King Lear]* That's a shealed peascod.

GONERIL: Not only, sir, this your all-licensed fool,
    But other of your insolent retinue
    Do hourly carp and quarrel; breaking forth
    In rank and not-to-be endured riots. Sir,
180   I had thought, by making this well known unto you,
    To have found a safe redress; but now grow fearful,
    By what yourself too late have spoke and done.
    That you protect this course, and put it on
    By your allowance; which if you should, the fault

[Speaks] *Please uncle, can you hire a teacher to teach your fool how to lie? I would much like to learn how to lie.*

KING LEAR: *If you do lie, sir, we'll have you whipped!*

FOOL: *I wonder how you and your daughters are related. They'll have me whipped for saying the truth, you'll have me whipped for lying, and, sometimes, I'm whipped for saying nothing. I'd rather be anything but a fool, and yet, I wouldn't want to be you, uncle. You have split your intelligence into two halves and left nothing in the middle. Here comes one of the halves.*

[Goneril enters]

KING LEAR: *What is it, daughter? Why are you frowning? I think you have been frowning too much lately.*

FOOL: *You were better off when you didn't have to care about her frowning. Now, you're just a worthless zero! I'm better than you are now. I'm a fool; you are nothing. [To Goneril] Yes, truly, I'll hold my tongue. Your facial expression tells me to do so, even though you haven't said anything.*
    Hush, hush. He who gives away the whole loaf will
    find himself wanting something. [He points to Lear]
    He is an empty pea pod.

GONERIL: *Sir, not only your privileged fool here, but others among your rude followers are complaining and fighting constantly, causing violent riots that cannot be endured. Sir, I thought that by informing you about this, the situation would be taken care of. But now, judging by what you yourself have recently said and done, I fear that you allow this kind of behavior and encourage it with your permission. If this is the case, your actions will not go uncriticized. Nor will the remedies rest that are necessary for the care of a well-ordered society, even if*

61

185   Would not 'scape censure, nor the redresses sleep,
Which, in the tender of a wholesome weal,
Might in their working do you that offence,
Which else were shame, that then necessity
Will call discreet proceeding.

190   FOOL: For, you trow, nuncle,
              The hedge-sparrow fed the cuckoo so long,
              That it's had it head bit off by it young.
    So, out went the candle, and we were left darkling.

KING LEAR: Are you our daughter?

195   GONERIL: Come, sir,
    I would you would make use of that good wisdom,
    Whereof I know you are fraught; and put away
    These dispositions, that of late transform you
    From what you rightly are.

200   FOOL: May not an ass know when the cart draws the horse? Whoop,
    Jug! I love thee.

KING LEAR: Doth any here know me? This is not Lear:
    Doth Lear walk thus? speak thus? Where are his eyes?
    Either his notion weakens, his discernings
205   Are lethargied—Ha! waking? 'tis not so.
    Who is it that can tell me who I am?

FOOL: Lear's shadow.

KING LEAR: I would learn that; for, by the marks of sovereignty,
    knowledge, and reason, I should be false persuaded I had
210   daughters.

FOOL: Which they will make an obedient father.

*they will offend you and might, under other circumstances, be
disgraceful to you.*

FOOL: *Because, you know, uncle,*
> *"The hedge-sparrow fed the cuckoo so long, that it
> had its head bit off by its young."*
So, the candle went out, and we were left in the dark.

KING LEAR: *Are you our daughter?*

GONERIL: *Come, sir, I wish you would use your sound sense, which I
know you possess, and that you would stop these tendencies that have
recently changed your identity.*

FOOL: *Cannot the fool see when the cart draws the horse? Gee, Jug! I
love you.*

KING LEAR: *Does anyone here recognize me? This is not Lear: Does Lear
walk this way? Speak this way? Where are his eyes? Either his intel-
lect weakens or his senses are clouded—what? Awake? That's not
the case. Is there anyone who can tell me who I am?*

FOOL: *Lear's shadow.*

KING LEAR: *I would like to know that, because my royal insignia,
my knowledge, and my reason would falsely tell me that I had
daughters.*

FOOL: *Who will make you into an obedient father.*

KING LEAR: Your name, fair gentlewoman?

GONERIL: This admiration, sir, is much o' the savour
    Of other your new pranks. I do beseech you
215   To understand my purposes aright:
    As you are old and reverend, you should be wise.
    Here do you keep a hundred knights and squires;
    Men so disorder'd, so debosh'd and bold,
    That this our court, infected with their manners,
220   Shows like a riotous inn: epicurism and lust
    Make it more like a tavern or a brothel
    Than a graced palace. The shame itself doth speak
    For instant remedy: be then desired
    By her, that else will take the thing she begs,
225   A little to disquantity your train;
    And the remainder, that shall still depend,
    To be such men as may besort your age,
    And know themselves and you.

230 KING LEAR: Darkness and devils!
    Saddle my horses; call my train together:
    Degenerate bastard! I'll not trouble thee.
    Yet have I left a daughter.

GONERIL: You strike my people; and your disorder'd rabble
235   Make servants of their betters.

[Enter Albany]

KING LEAR: Woe, that too late repents,— *[To Albany]*
    O, sir, are you come?
    Is it your will? Speak, sir. Prepare my horses.
    Ingratitude, thou marble-hearted fiend,
240   More hideous when thou show'st thee in a child
    Than the sea-monster!

ALBANY: Pray, sir, be patient.

KING LEAR: *What is your name, fair gentlewoman?*

GONERIL: *This pretended astonishment, sir, is very much like your other new pranks. I am asking you to understand my intentions correctly. You should be as wise as your are old and respected. You keep here a hundred knights and squires, men so disorderly, immoral, and daring that our entire court has been contaminated by their bad manners and resembles a rowdy inn. Excessive living and lust make it more like a tavern or a brothel than a dignified palace. This disgrace demands an instant resolution. I request—or else will take what I am asking for—that you reduce the number of your followers. And the rest who will stay and continue to depend on you should be men appropriate to your age who know how they and you should behave.*

KING LEAR: *Darkness and devils! Saddle my horse; gather my troops together. Immoral bastard! I will not trouble you; I have yet one more daughter left.*

GONERIL: *You strike my attendants, and your disorderly men treat their superiors like servants.*

[Albany enters]

KING LEAR: *Woe to him who repents too late—* [To Albany] *Oh, sir, are you here? Is this what you want? Speak, sir. Prepare my horses. Ingratitude, you're a beast with a heart of stone, more hideous when you appear in a child than in a sea-monster.*

ALBANY: *I beg you, sir, calm down.*

KING LEAR: *[To Goneril]* Detested kite! thou liest.
 My train are men of choice and rarest parts,
245 That all particulars of duty know,
 And in the most exact regard support
 The worships of their name. O most small fault,
 How ugly didst thou in Cordelia show!
 That, like an engine, wrench'd my frame of nature
250 From the fix'd place; drew from heart all love,
 And added to the gall. O Lear, Lear, Lear!
 Beat at this gate, that let thy folly in, *[Striking his head]*
 And thy dear judgment out! Go, go, my people.

ALBANY: My lord, I am guiltless, as I am ignorant
255 Of what hath moved you.

KING LEAR: It may be so, my lord.
 Hear, nature, hear; dear goddess, hear!
 Suspend thy purpose, if thou didst intend
 To make this creature fruitful!
260 Into her womb convey sterility!
 Dry up in her the organs of increase;
 And from her derogate body never spring
 A babe to honour her! If she must teem,
 Create her child of spleen; that it may live,
265 And be a thwart disnatured torment to her!
 Let it stamp wrinkles in her brow of youth;
 With cadent tears fret channels in her cheeks;
 Turn all her mother's pains and benefits
 To laughter and contempt; that she may feel
270 How sharper than a serpent's tooth it is
 To have a thankless child! Away, away! *[Exit]*

ALBANY: Now, gods that we adore, whereof comes this?

GONERIL: Never afflict yourself to know the cause;
 But let his disposition have that scope
275 That dotage gives it.

KING LEAR: [To Goneril] *You predator! You lie. My troops consist of men with excellent and extraordinary qualities, who know their duties well and carefully uphold their honorable reputations. Oh, how the smallest fault seemed monstrous in Cordelia. It tore me apart, drew all my love from my heart and caused me bitterness. Oh Lear, Lear, Lear! Strike at this door that let foolishness in and kept sound reasoning out. [He strikes his head] Go, go my people!*

ALBANY: *My lord, I am innocent because I don't know what has made you angry.*

KING LEAR: *That may be the case, my lord. Hear, Nature, hear. Dear goddess, hear. Change your mind if you had intended this creature to be fertile. Make her sterile! Dry up her reproductive organs so that her detestable body may never honor her with a baby. If she must give birth, fill her child with spitefulness, so that it may live to be a perverse, ungrateful torment to her! Let it force wrinkles onto her youthful face and let tears cut channels into her cheeks. Turn all her maternal care into mockery and contempt, so that she will feel how much more painful than a snakebite it is to have a thankless child. Come away, away.*

[Lear exits]

ALBANY: *Oh mighty gods, what brought this on?*

GONERIL: *Don't worry about the cause, but let his behavior live up to his old age.*

[Re-enter King Lear]

KING LEAR: What, fifty of my followers at a clap!
    Within a fortnight!

ALBANY: What's the matter, sir?

KING LEAR: I'll tell thee: *[To Goneril]* Life and death! I am ashamed
280   That thou hast power to shake my manhood thus;
    That these hot tears, which break from me perforce,
    Should make thee worth them. Blasts and fogs upon thee!
    The untented woundings of a father's curse
    Pierce every sense about thee! Old fond eyes,
285   Beweep this cause again, I'll pluck ye out,
    And cast you, with the waters that you lose,
    To temper clay. Yea, it is come to this?
    Let is be so: yet have I left a daughter,
    Who, I am sure, is kind and comfortable:
290   When she shall hear this of thee, with her nails
    She'll flay thy wolvish visage. Thou shalt find
    That I'll resume the shape which thou dost think
    I have cast off for ever: thou shalt,
    I warrant thee.

[Exeunt King Lear, Kent, and Attendants]

295   **GONERIL:** Do you mark that, my lord?

ALBANY: I cannot be so partial, Goneril,
    To the great love I bear you,—

GONERIL: Pray you, content. What, Oswald, ho!
    [To the Fool] You, sir, more knave than fool, after your master.

[Lear enters]

KING LEAR: *What, fifty of my followers at once? Within two weeks?*

ALBANY: *What's the matter, sir?*

KING LEAR: *I'll tell you.* [To Goneril] *By my life, I am ashamed that you have the power to tear down my strengths this way. These tears I shed now have more value than you do. Curses and blindness on you! These deep wounds I wish for you shall stab you in everywhere. My eyes, if you ever weep again for this reason, I'll pluck you from my head and throw you into the ocean you cause and make clay. Ha! Has it become this? Fine. I have one daughter left who is kind and helpful. When she hears what you've done, she'll scratch your ugly face with her nails. You'll see that I will resume the position that you thought I had given up forever. You will, I guarantee it!*

[Lear, Kent, and Attendants exit]

GONERIL: *Did you hear that, my lord?*

ALBANY: *I cannot be so unfair, despite the deep love I feel for you, to—*

GONERIL: *Please be quiet! What, Oswald, hey!* [To the Fool] *You, sir, more scoundrel than a fool, follow your master.*

300 FOOL: Nuncle Lear, nuncle Lear, tarry and take the fool with thee.
    A fox, when one has caught her,
    And such a daughter,
    Should sure to the slaughter,
    If my cap would buy a halter:
305   So the fool follows after.   *[Exit]*

GONERIL: This man hath had good counsel:—a hundred knights!
  'Tis politic and safe to let him keep
  At point a hundred knights: yes, that, on every dream,
  Each buzz, each fancy, each complaint, dislike,
310   He may enguard his dotage with their powers,
  And hold our lives in mercy. Oswald, I say!

ALBANY: Well, you may fear too far.

GONERIL: Safer than trust too far:
  Let me still take away the harms I fear,
315   Not fear still to be taken: I know his heart.
  What he hath utter'd I have writ my sister
  If she sustain him and his hundred knights
  When I have show'd the unfitness,—

[Re-enter Oswald]

        How now, Oswald!
320   What, have you writ that letter to my sister?

OSWALD: Yes, madam.

GONERIL: Take you some company, and away to horse:
  Inform her full of my particular fear;
  And thereto add such reasons of your own
325   As may compact it more. Get you gone;
  And hasten your return. *[Exit Oswald]* No, no, my lord,
  This milky gentleness and course of yours
  Though I condemn not, yet, under pardon,
  You are much more attask'd for want of wisdom
330   Than praised for harmful mildness.

70

FOOL: *Uncle Lear, uncle Lear, please take the fool with you.*
        A fox when you have caught her, and such a daughter,
        should surely be brought to the slaughterhouse, if my
        cap would buy a halter. So, the fool follows.

[Fool exits]

GONERIL: *This man (Lear) has good judgment. A hundred knights! It is wise and safe to let him keep a hundred armed knights! Yes, so that after every dream, rumor, fantasy, complaint, or dislike he can protect his senility with their power and hold our lives under his control. Oswald, I say.*

ALBANY: *Well, you might fear too much.*

GONERIL: *Safer than trust too much. Allow me to eliminate the dangers that I fear rather than to worry constantly about harmful consequences. I know him well. I have written to my sister about what he has said. If she maintains him and his hundred knights, after I have emphasized the inappropriateness—*

[Oswald reenters]

How are things, Oswald? Have you written that letter to my sister?

OSWALD: *Yes, madam.*

GONERIL: *Take some companions and ride off. Tell her all about my personal fears. Add any of your own reasons that might validate my worries. Get going, and hurry back soon .*

[Oswald exits]

No, no, my lord. I don't condemn your mild and gentle attitude, but, if I may say so, you will be criticized much more for your lack of wisdom than you will be praised for your harmful leniency.

71

ALBANY: How far your eyes may pierce I can not tell:
   Striving to better, oft we mar what's well.

GONERIL: Nay, then—

ALBANY: Well, well; the event.   *[Exeunt]*

SCENE V

Court before the same.

[Enter King Lear, Kent, and Fool]

KING LEAR: Go you before to Gloucester with these letters.
   Acquaint my daughter no further with any thing you
   know than comes from her demand out of the letter.
   If your diligence be not speedy, I shall be there afore you.

5   KENT: I will not sleep, my lord, till I have delivered your letter.
                                          [Exit]

FOOL: If a man's brains were in's heels, were't not in danger of
   kibes?

KING LEAR: Ay, boy.

FOOL: Then, I prithee, be merry; thy wit shall ne'er go slip-shod.

10   KING LEAR: Ha, ha, ha!

ALBANY: In how far you might be right, I'm not sure. Sometimes we ruin a good thing, when we try too hard to make it better.

GONERIL: Well, then—

ALBANY: Well, well, we'll see how things turn out.   [They exit]

SCENE V

The court before Albany's palace.

[Lear, Kent, disguised, and Fool enter]

KING LEAR: You go ahead to the city of Gloucester with this letter. Tell my daughter no more than necessary in order to answer questions arising from the letter. If you don't act quickly, I'll be there before you.

KENT: I will not sleep, my lord, until I have delivered your letter.
                                        [Kent exits]

FOOL: If a man's brains were in his shoes, would they not be in danger of chilblains?

KING LEAR: Yes, boy.

FOOL: Well, then, be happy. You'll never need to wear slippers to protect your intelligence.

KING LEAR: Ha, ha, ha!

Fool: Shalt see thy other daughter will use thee kindly; for though she's as like this as a crab's like an apple, yet I can tell what I can tell.

King Lear: Why, what canst thou tell, my boy?

15 Fool: She will taste as like this as a crab does to a crab. Thou canst tell why one's nose stands i' the middle on's face?

King Lear: No.

Fool: Why, to keep one's eyes of either side's nose; that what a man cannot smell out, he may spy into.

20 King Lear: I did her wrong—

Fool: Canst tell how an oyster makes his shell?

King Lear: No.

Fool: Nor I neither; but I can tell why a snail has a house.

King Lear: Why?

25 Fool: Why, to put his head in; not to give it away to his daughters, and leave his horns without a case.

King Lear: I will forget my nature. So kind a father! Be my horses ready?

Fool: Thy asses are gone about 'em. The reason why the seven stars are no more than seven is a pretty reason.

King Lear: Because they are not eight?

FOOL: *You'll see that your other daughter will treat you nicely. Though she's as like this one as a crabapple is like an apple; I know what I know.*

KING LEAR: *What do you know, my boy?*

FOOL: *She will taste as much like this one, as a crabapple tastes like a crabapple. Do you know why one's nose sits in the center of the face?*

KING LEAR: *No.*

FOOL: *Well, to keep one eye on either side of the nose, so that a man can see what he can't smell.*

KING LEAR: *I wronged her (Cordelia).*

FOOL: *Do you know why an oyster makes its shell?*

KING LEAR: *No.*

FOOL: *I don't either. But I know why a snail has a house.*

KING LEAR: *Why?*

FOOL: *To put its head inside, of course, so he doesn't give it away to his daughters and leave himself unprotected.*

KING LEAR: *I'll forget my natural affection. Such a kind father. Are my horses ready?*

FOOL: *Your foolish servants are getting them ready. There's a good reason why the Pleiades are only seven stars.*

KING LEAR: *Because they don't have eight?*

FOOL: Yes, indeed: thou wouldst make a good fool.

KING LEAR: To take 't again perforce! Monster ingratitude!

FOOL: If thou wert my fool, nuncle, I'd have thee beaten for being
    old before thy time.

35 KING LEAR: How's that?

FOOL: Thou shouldst not have been old till thou hadst been wise.

KING LEAR: O, let me not be mad, not mad, sweet heaven
    Keep me in temper: I would not be mad!

[Enter Gentleman]
    How now! are the horses ready?

40 GENTLEMAN: Ready, my lord.

KING LEAR: Come, boy.

FOOL: She that's a maid now, and laughs at my departure,
    Shall not be a maid long, unless things be cut shorter.

                                                    [Exeunt]

FOOL: *Yes, indeed. You would make a good fool!*

KING LEAR: [Thinking about reclaiming his throne] *To take it back by force! Ingratitude, you monster!*

FOOL: *If you were my fool, uncle, I'd have you beaten for acting older than you are.*

KING LEAR: *How's that possible?*

FOOL: *You shouldn't have grown old until you'd grown wise.*

KING LEAR: *Oh, let me not go mad, not mad, sweet heaven; let me keep my mental balance! I don't want to be mad!*

[A Gentleman enters]
   Well, are the horses ready?

GENTLEMAN: *Ready, my lord.*

KING LEAR: [To the Fool] *Come, boy.*

FOOL: *A virgin who laughs at our prospective future won't stay a virgin for long, because she must be very simple-minded!*

[They exit]

ACT II

SCENE I

Gloucester's castle.

[Enter Edmund, and Curan meets him]

EDMUND: Save thee, Curan.

CURAN: And you, sir. I have been with your father, and given him notice that the Duke of Cornwall and Regan his duchess will be here with him this night.

EDMUND: How comes that?

5   CURAN: Nay, I know not. You have heard of the news abroad; I mean the whispered ones, for they are yet but ear-kissing arguments?

EDMUND: Not I pray you, what are they?

CURAN: Have you heard of no likely wars toward, 'twixt the Dukes of Cornwall and Albany?

10   EDMUND: Not a word.

CURAN: You may do, then, in time. Fare you well, sir.

[Exit]

ACT II

SCENE I

Gloucester's castle.

[Edmund and Curan enter]

EDMUND: *May God be with you, Curan.*

CURAN: *And with you, sir. I have been at your father's house and have informed him that the Duke of Cornwall and Regan, his Duchess, will be here with him tonight.*

EDMUND: *How come?*

CURAN: *Well, I don't know. I'm sure you've heard of the latest news? I mean the rumors that are just beginning to go around?*

EDMUND: *I haven't. Tell me, what are they?*

CURAN: *Haven't you heard about the impending war between the Duke of Cornwall and the Duke of Albany?*

EDMUND: *Not a word.*

CURAN: *You will in time. Farewell, sir.*

[Curan exits]

EDMUND: The duke be here to-night? The better! best!
    This weaves itself perforce into my business.
    My father hath set guard to take my brother;
15   And I have one thing, of a queasy question,
    Which I must act: briefness and fortune, work!
    Brother, a word; descend: brother, I say!

[Enter Edgar]
    My father watches: O sir, fly this place;
20   Intelligence is given where you are hid;
    You have now the good advantage of the night:
    Have you not spoken 'gainst the Duke of Cornwall?
    He's coming hither: now, i' the night, i' the haste,
    And Regan with him: have you nothing said
25   Upon his party 'gainst the Duke of Albany?
    Advise yourself.

EDGAR: I am sure on't, not a word.

EDMUND: I hear my father coming: pardon me:
    In cunning I must draw my sword upon you
30   Draw; seem to defend yourself; now quit you well.
    Yield: come before my father. Light, ho, here!
    Fly, brother. Torches, torches! So, farewell.

                          [Exit Edgar]
    Some blood drawn on me would beget opinion.
                      [Wounds his arm]
    Of my more fierce endeavour: I have seen drunkards
35   Do more than this in sport. Father, father!
    Stop, stop! No help?

[Enter Gloucester, and Servants with torches]

GLOUCESTER: Now, Edmund, where's the villain?

EDMUND: Here stood he in the dark, his sharp sword out,
    Mumbling of wicked charms, conjuring the moon
40   To stand auspicious mistress,—

80

EDMUND: *The duke will be here tonight? Great! Fantastic! This fits perfectly into my plan! My father has prepared to spy on my brother, and I have something of a delicate nature that I have to take care of. Speed and good fortune must work!* [Calling upstairs] *Brother, I must have a word with you. Come down, brother.*

[Edgar enters]

My father is watching. Oh sir, flee from here. Your hiding place has been revealed. Now you are protected by night. Have you not said anything against the Duke of Cornwall? He's coming here, right now, in the middle of the night, in a rush. And Regan is with him. Have you not said anything about him against the Duke of Albany? Consider it carefully.

EDGAR: *I'm certain. Not a word.*

EDMUND: *I hear my father coming. Forgive me; I must pretend to draw my sword on you.* [To Edgar] *Draw your sword. Pretend to defend yourself. Now do your part.*
[Loudly, so Gloucester can hear] *Surrender. Show yourself to my father. Light, here.*
[Whispering to Edgar] *Run, brother!*
[Loudly] *Torches. Torches.*
[To Edgar] *So, farewell.*
[Edgar exits]
Some blood on me would give the impression that I fought fiercely [He wounds himself] *I have seen drunkards do worse than this for fun. Father, father! Stop, stop! No help?*

[Gloucester and Servants enter carrying torches]

GLOUCESTER: *Well, Edmund, where's the villain?*

EDMUND: *He stood here in the dark, with his sharp sword drawn, mumbling wicked spells, and calling to the moon for assistance.*

81

GLOUCESTER: But where is he?

EDMUND: Look, sir, I bleed.

GLOUCESTER: Where is the villain, Edmund?

EDMUND: Fled this way, sir. When by no means he could—

45 GLOUCESTER: Pursue him, ho! Go after. *[Exeunt some Servants]*
       By no means what?

EDMUND: Persuade me to the murder of your lordship;
       But that I told him, the revenging gods
       'Gainst parricides did all their thunders bend;
50   Spoke, with how manifold and strong a bond
       The child was bound to the father; sir, in fine,
       Seeing how loathly opposite I stood
       To his unnatural purpose, in fell motion,
       With his prepared sword, he charges home
55   My unprovided body, lanced mine arm:
       But when he saw my best alarum'd spirits,
       Bold in the quarrel's right, roused to the encounter,
       Or whether gasted by the noise I made,
       Full suddenly he fled.

60 GLOUCESTER: Let him fly far:
       Not in this land shall he remain uncaught;
       And found—dispatch. The noble duke my master,
       My worthy arch and patron, comes to-night:
       By his authority I will proclaim it,
65   That he which finds him shall deserve our thanks,
       Bringing the murderous coward to the stake;
       He that conceals him, death.

EDMUND: When I dissuaded him from his intent,
       And found him pight to do it, with curst speech
70   I threaten'd to discover him: he replied,

GLOUCESTER: *But where is he now?*

EDMUND: *Look sir, I'm bleeding!*

GLOUCESTER: *Where is the villain, Edmund?*

EDMUND: *He fled this way, sir, when he wasn't able to—*

GLOUCESTER: *Chase him! Quick, go after him!* [Some Servants exit]
   "wasn't able to" do what?

EDMUND: *Persuade me to kill your lordship. And I told him that the angry
   gods aim their thunderbolts at parricides and then explained how
   intricate and strong the bond is that connects the child to his father.
   Sir, in short, when he saw how steadfastly I opposed his despicable
   plan, he aimed directly at my unprotected body with a fierce thrust
   and wounded my arm. But when he saw my finest courage roused to
   action, confident in the justice of the cause, or perhaps frightened of
   the noise I made, he suddenly fled.*

GLOUCESTER: *Let him run off. If he is in this land, he will be caught!
   Once he has been found—kill him! My master, the noble Duke,
   my worthy chief patron, will arrive tonight. By his authority, I
   will proclaim that he who finds him will receive a reward for
   bringing the murderous coward to his execution. If anyone hides
   him, death!*

EDMUND: *When I tried to dissuade him from his plan, and found that
   he was determined to go through with it, I threatened, with angry
   words, to reveal his plan. He replied: "You poor bastard! Do you*

83

'Thou unpossessing bastard! dost thou think,
If I would stand against thee, would the reposal
Of any trust, virtue, or worth in thee
Make thy words faith'd? No: what I should deny,—
75   As this I would: ay, though thou didst produce
My very character,—I'd turn it all
To thy suggestion, plot, and damned practise:
And thou must make a dullard of the world,
If they not thought the profits of my death
80   Were very pregnant and potential spurs
To make thee seek it.'

GLOUCESTER: Strong and fasten'd villain
Would he deny his letter? I never got him.
                                        [Tucket within]
Hark, the duke's trumpets! I know not why he comes.
85   All ports I'll bar; the villain shall not 'scape;
The duke must grant me that: besides, his picture
I will send far and near, that all the kingdom
May have the due note of him; and of my land,
Loyal and natural boy, I'll work the means
90   To make thee capable.

[Enter Cornwall, Regan, and Attendants]

CORNWALL: How now, my noble friend! since I came hither,
Which I can call but now, I have heard strange news.

REGAN: If it be true, all vengeance comes too short
Which can pursue the offender. How dost, my lord?

95   GLOUCESTER: O, madam, my old heart is crack'd, it's crack'd!

REGAN: What, did my father's godson seek your life?
He whom my father named? your Edgar?

GLOUCESTER: O, lady, lady, shame would have it hid!

think that any trust our father could place in you, any virtue or merit, would make anybody believe your words if I opposed them? No! I would deny everything, even if you could produce evidence in my own handwriting. I would blame it all on your evil plan, your plotting and treacherous scheming. And you must think people very stupid if you don't understand that they'd think the profits from my death were a compelling and powerful incentive for you to seek it.

GLOUCESTER: That strong and confirmed villain! Would he deny this letter? He is not my child! [A trumpet is heard] Hear. The duke's trumpets. I don't know why he's coming here. I'll block all gates. The villain must not escape! The duke must allow me to do that. Besides, I'll send a description of him everywhere, so that the entire kingdom will take note of him. [To Edmund] And as far as my land is concerned, my loyal and true son, I'll make sure that you will legally inherit it.

Turning on child much like lear.

[Cornwall, Regan, and Attendants enter]

CORNWALL: How are you, my noble friend? I have just arrived here, but I have heard strange news.

REGAN: If it's true, no revenge is enough in pursuing the offender. How are you, my lord?

Revenge on family

GLOUCESTER: Oh, madam, my old heart has been broken, broken.

REGAN: What, did my father's godson try to kill you? The one my father named? Your son Edgar?

GLOUCESTER: Oh, lady, lady. I should not admit it due to the shame that comes with it.

REGAN: Was he not companion with the riotous knights
100   That tend upon my father?

GLOUCESTER: I know not, madam: 'tis too bad, too bad.

EDMUND: Yes, madam, he was of that consort.

REGAN: No marvel, then, though he were ill affected:
     'Tis they have put him on the old man's death,
105   To have the expense and waste of his revenues.
     I have this present evening from my sister
     Been well inform'd of them; and with such cautions,
     That if they come to sojourn at my house,
     I'll not be there.

110 CORNWALL: Nor I, assure thee, Regan.
     Edmund, I hear that you have shown your father
     A child-like office.

EDMUND: 'Twas my duty, sir.

115 GLOUCESTER: He did bewray his practise; and received
     This hurt you see, striving to apprehend him.

CORNWALL: Is he pursued?

GLOUCESTER: Ay, my good lord.

CORNWALL: If he be taken, he shall never more
     Be fear'd of doing harm: make your own purpose,
120   How in my strength you please. For you, Edmund,
     Whose virtue and obedience doth this instant
     So much commend itself, you shall be ours:
     Natures of such deep trust we shall much need;
     You we first seize on.

REGAN: *Wasn't he a companion of the riotous knights who serve my father?*

GLOUCESTER: *I don't know, madam. It is too bad, too bad!*

EDMUND: *Yes, madam, he belonged to that gang.*

REGAN: *It's no wonder then, that he was given to evil ways. They have incited him to plan the old man's death, so that they can waste his wealth. I have been informed about them by my sister this very evening. I received such warnings that if they come to stay at my house, I won't be there.*

CORNWALL: *Neither will I, I assure you, Regan. Edmund, I hear that you have provided your father with the help that is proper to a son.*

EDMUND: *It was my duty, sir.*

GLOUCESTER: *He revealed Edgar's plan, sir, and received this wound* [pointing to Edgar's arm] *while trying to arrest him.*

CORNWALL: *Is he being pursued?*

GLOUCESTER: *Yes, my good lord.*

CORNWALL: *When he's captured, nobody must ever fear any harm from him again. By my authority, do as you please with him! As to you, Edmund, your virtue and obedience speak for themselves. You shall be one of us. We will need trustworthy natures. We take up your services right away.*

125 EDMUND: I shall serve you, sir,
     Truly, however else.

GLOUCESTER: For him I thank your grace.

CORNWALL: You know not why we came to visit you,—

REGAN: Thus out of season, threading dark-eyed night:
130   Occasions, noble Gloucester, of some poise,
        Wherein we must have use of your advice:
        Our father he hath writ, so hath our sister,
        Of differences, which I least thought it fit
        To answer from our home; the several messengers
135   From hence attend dispatch. Our good old friend,
        Lay comforts to your bosom; and bestow
        Your needful counsel to our business,
        Which craves the instant use.

GLOUCESTER: I serve you, madam:
140   Your graces are right welcome.   [Exeunt]

SCENE II

Before Gloucester's castle.

[Enter Kent and Oswald, severally]

OSWALD: Good dawning to thee, friend: art of this house?

KENT: Ay.

OSWALD: Where may we set our horses?

EDMUND: *I will serve you, sir. Truly, in any way.*

GLOUCESTER: *On his behalf, I thank your Grace.*

CORNWALL: *You don't know why we came to visit you.*

REGAN: *So unexpectedly, undertaking a difficult passage through the pitch-black night. We need your advice, noble Gloucester, in matters of great importance. Our father has written us, and so has our sister, about certain difficulties that I did not want to address from home. Several messengers are waiting to be sent back. Our good old friend! Be comforted and give your much-needed advice to our situation, which requires immediate attention.*

GLOUCESTER: *I serve you, madam. Your Graces are most welcome.*

[A trumpet sounds. All exit]

SCENE II

Before Gloucester's castle.

[Kent (in disguise) and Oswald enter separately]

OSWALD: *Good morning to you, my friend. Do you belong to this house?*

KENT: *Yes.*

OSWALD: *Where may we leave our horses?*

KENT: I' the mire.

5   OSWALD: Prithee, if thou lovest me, tell me.

KENT: I love thee not.

OSWALD: Why, then, I care not for thee.

KENT: If I had thee in Lipsbury pinfold, I would make thee care for
    me.

10   OSWALD: Why dost thou use me thus? I know thee not.

KENT: Fellow, I know thee.

OSWALD: What dost thou know me for?

KENT: A knave; a rascal; an eater of broken meats; a base, proud,
    shallow, beggarly, three-suited, hundred-pound, filthy, worsted-
15   stocking knave; a lily-livered, action-taking knave, a whoreson,
    glass-gazing, super-serviceable finical rogue; one-trunk-inherit-
    ing slave; one that wouldst be a bawd, in way of good service,
    and art nothing but the composition of a knave, beggar, coward,
    pandar, and the son and heir of a mongrel bitch: one whom I
20   will beat into clamorous whining, if thou deniest the least syl-
    lable of thy addition.

OSWALD: Why, what a monstrous fellow art thou, thus to rail on one
    that is neither known of thee nor knows thee!

KENT: What a brazen-faced varlet art thou, to deny thou knowest
25   me! Is it two days ago since I tripped up thy heels, and beat
    thee before the king? Draw, you rogue: for, though it be night,
    yet the moon shines; I'll make a sop o' the moonshine of you:
    draw, you whoreson cullionly barber-monger, draw.
                          [Drawing his sword]

KENT: *In the mud.*

OSWALD: *Please, if you love me, tell me.*

KENT: *I don't love you.*

OSWALD: *Then I don't care about you.*

KENT: *If I had you between my teeth, I would make you care for me.*

OSWALD: *Why do you treat me like that? I don't know you.*

KENT: *But I know you, fellow!*

OSWALD: *What do you know about me?*

KENT: *You're a scoundrel, a rascal, a dirt eater, a primitive, proud, shallow, beggarly, pretentious, scoundrel! A cowardly scoundrel, a vain bastard, a self-important, affected rogue, and a poor slave! One who considers manipulation to be a part of his duties. You are nothing but the combination of a scoundrel, beggar, coward, manipulator, and the son and heir of a mongrel bitch. A man I will beat till he whines, if he denies any of the things I have said about him.*

based off gossip

OSWALD: *What kind of monster are you? To talk this way about someone you don't know and who doesn't know you.*

KENT: *What a shameless rogue are you, to deny that you know me. Has it been two days yet, since I tripped your feet and beat you in front of the king? Draw your sword, you rogue! Even though it's night-time, the moon is shining, I'll pierce your body so the moonshine shines through. Draw your sword, you despicable fop!* [He draws his sword]

91

OSWALD: Away! I have nothing to do with thee.

30 KENT: Draw, you rascal: you come with letters against the king; and take vanity the puppet's part against the royalty of her father: draw, you rogue, or I'll so carbonado your shanks: draw, you rascal; come your ways.

OSWALD: Help, ho! murder! help!

35 KENT: Strike, you slave; stand, rogue, stand; you neat slave, strike.
[Beating him]

OSWALD: Help, ho! murder! murder!

[Enter Edmund, with his rapier drawn, Cornwall, Regan, Gloucester, and Servants]

EDMUND: How now! What's the matter? Part.

KENT: With you, goodman boy, an you please: come, I'll flesh ye; come on, young master.

40 GLOUCESTER: Weapons! arms! What's the matter here?

CORNWALL: Keep peace, upon your lives:
He dies that strikes again. What is the matter?

REGAN: The messengers from our sister and the king.

CORNWALL: What is your difference? speak.

45 OSWALD: I am scarce in breath, my lord.

KENT: No marvel, you have so bestirred your valour. You cowardly rascal, nature disclaims in thee: a tailor made thee.

OSWALD: *Go away. I don't want to have anything to do with you.*

KENT: *Draw your sword, your rascal! You bring letters that speak out against the king, and you side with the vain Goneril against her royal father. Draw, you rogue, or I'll slash your body! Draw, you rascal, come on!*

kent has anger
FOR
the king

OSWALD: *Help! Hello! Murder! Help!*

KENT: *Fight, you slave; stand your ground, rogue! You pretentious slave, fight!* [He beats on him]

OSWALD: *Help! Hello! Murder! Help!*

[Edmund enters with his rapier drawn. Cornwall, Regan, Gloucester, and Servants enter]

EDMUND: *What is going on? What's the matter?* [He parts them]

KENT: *I'll take you on, you youngster, if you please! Come on, I'll show you how to fight! Come on, young master!*

GLOUCESTER: *Weapons! Arms! What's the matter here?*

CORNWALL: *Be peaceful, upon your lives! The one who strikes one more time will die. What's the matter?*

REGAN: *These are the messengers from our sister and the king.*

CORNWALL: *What is the trouble? Explain.*

OSWALD: *I have to catch my breath, my lord.*

KENT: *No wonder; you have disturbed your courage. You -cowardly rascal, Nature denies she created you; you were made by a tailor.*

93

CORNWALL: Thou art a strange fellow: a tailor make a man?

KENT: Ay, a tailor, sir: a stone-cutter or painter could not have made
50   him so ill, though he had been but two hours at the trade.

CORNWALL: Speak yet, how grew your quarrel?

OSWALD: This ancient ruffian, sir, whose life I have spared at suit of
       his gray beard,—

KENT: Thou whoreson zed! thou unnecessary letter! My lord, if you
55   will give me leave, I will tread this unbolted villain into mortar,
       and daub the wall of a jakes with him. Spare my gray beard, you
       wagtail?

CORNWALL: Peace, sirrah!
       You beastly knave, know you no reverence?

60   KENT: Yes, sir; but anger hath a privilege.

CORNWALL: Why art thou angry?

KENT: That such a slave as this should wear a sword,
       Who wears no honesty. Such smiling rogues as these,
       Like rats, oft bite the holy cords a-twain
65   Which are too intrinse to unloose; smooth every passion
       That in the natures of their lords rebel;
       Bring oil to fire, snow to their colder moods;
       Renege, affirm, and turn their halcyon beaks
       With every gale and vary of their masters,
70   Knowing nought, like dogs, but following.
       A plague upon your epileptic visage!
       Smile you my speeches, as I were a fool?
       Goose, if I had you upon Sarum plain,
       I'd drive ye cackling home to Camelot.

CORNWALL: *You are a strange man. A tailor can make a man?*

KENT: *Yes, a tailor, sir! A stone cutter or a painter wouldn't have done such a bad job, even if he had only been in his profession for a couple of years.*

CORNWALL: *Still, explain. How did your quarrel start?*

OSWALD: *This old thug, whose life I have spared because of his grey beard—*

KENT: *You useless bastard! You unnecessary creature. My lord, if you will allow me, I will work this coarse villain into mortar and plaster the walls of a privy with him. Spare my gray beard, you slave!*

CORNWALL: *Peace, sir. You irreverent scoundrel! Don't you have any respect?*

KENT: *Yes, sir, but anger comes first.*

CORNWALL: *Why are you angry?*

KENT: *Because a slave like this one can wear a sword, though he does not possess an honorable character. Smiling rogues like these often—like rats—bite through the holy bond between father and child that, otherwise, is too tight to be undone. They satisfy their masters' inappropriate passions, fuel any anger, add chills to their sadness, deny, affirm, and support the changing moods of their masters. Like dogs, knowing nothing but how to follow. I curse your twitching face! Do you smile at what I say, as if I am a fool? You goose! If I had you on Salisbury Plain, I'd send you home running!*

75 CORNWALL: Why, art thou mad, old fellow?

GLOUCESTER: How fell you out? say that.

KENT: No contraries hold more antipathy
    Than I and such a knave.

CORNWALL: Why dost thou call him a knave? What's his offence?

80 KENT: His countenance likes me not.

CORNWALL: No more, perchance, does mine, nor his, nor hers.

KENT: Sir, 'tis my occupation to be plain:
    I have seen better faces in my time
    Than stands on any shoulder that I see
85   Before me at this instant.

CORNWALL: This is some fellow,
    Who, having been praised for bluntness, doth affect
    A saucy roughness, and constrains the garb
    Quite from his nature: he cannot flatter, he,
90   An honest mind and plain, he must speak truth!
    An they will take it, so; if not, he's plain.
    These kind of knaves I know, which in this plainness
    Harbour more craft and more corrupter ends
    Than twenty silly ducking observants
95   That stretch their duties nicely.

KENT: Sir, in good sooth, in sincere verity,
    Under the allowance of your great aspect,
    Whose influence, like the wreath of radiant fire
    On flickering Phoebus' front,—

100 CORNWALL: What mean'st by this?

CORNWALL: *What, are you mad, old man?*

GLOUCESTER: *How did your fight start, explain that.*

KENT: *No two adversaries hate each other more than I and this scoundrel!*

CORNWALL: *Why do you call him scoundrel? What is his fault?*

KENT: *I don't like his face!*

CORNWALL: *Or mine, or his, or hers, perhaps!*

KENT: *Sir, it is my habit to be clear: I have seen better faces in my time than sit on any of the shoulders that I see here right now.*

CORNWALL: *This is some fellow, who, having been praised for bluntness, displays an insolent attitude and uses his frankness to conceal his deceitful nature. [Sarcastically] He can't flatter, being a plain and honest mind, he must speak the truth. If people accept it, fine. If not, that's just the way he is—plain. I know these kinds of scoundrels who, behind their frankness, disguise their skills and corrupt intentions better than twenty obedient servants who only live to fulfill their duties.*

KENT: *[Mockingly flattering] Sir, in all truth and honesty, given the approval of your great mind, whose power, like the ring of fire around the sun—*

CORNWALL: *What do you mean by this?*

KENT: To go out of my dialect, which you discommend so much.
   I know, sir, I am no flatterer: he that beguiled you in a plain
   accent was a plain knave; which for my part I will not be,
   though I should win your displeasure to entreat me to 't.

105 CORNWALL: What was the offence you gave him?

OSWALD: I never gave him any:
   It pleased the king his master very late
   To strike at me, upon his misconstruction;
   When he, conjunct and flattering his displeasure,
110 Tripp'd me behind; being down, insulted, rail'd,
   And put upon him such a deal of man,
   That worthied him, got praises of the king
   For him attempting who was self-subdued;
   And, in the fleshment of this dread exploit,
115 Drew on me here again.

KENT: None of these rogues and cowards
   But Ajax is their fool.

CORNWALL: Fetch forth the stocks!
   You stubborn ancient knave, you reverend braggart,
120 We'll teach you—

KENT: Sir, I am too old to learn:
   Call not your stocks for me: I serve the king;
   On whose employment I was sent to you:
   You shall do small respect, show too bold malice
125 Against the grace and person of my master,
   Stocking his messenger.

CORNWALL: Fetch forth the stocks! As I have life and honour,
   There shall he sit till noon.

REGAN: Till noon! till night, my lord; and all night too.

KENT: [In a normal tone] *I mean to change my way of speaking, which you dislike so much. I know, sir, that I'm no flatterer. The man whose plain speaking formed your opinion about bluntness was a plain scoundrel. That, I'll never be, though I might risk your displeasure if you begged me to be one and I refused.*

CORNWALL: [To Oswald] *How did you offend him?*

OSWALD: *I never offended him. The king, his master, recently decided to strike me after a misunderstanding, when he took the king's side, fueled his displeasure, and tripped me from behind. While I was down, he insulted me, screamed, and made himself seem like a valuable hero, so that he received praise from the king for attacking a man who offered no resistance. Excited by this terrible accomplishment, he drew his sword on me here again.*

KENT: *Scoundrels and villains like these always brag that they're braver than Ajax.*

CORNWALL: *Bring the stocks and tie him up. You stubborn old scoundrel! You aged blowhard! We'll teach you!*

KENT: *Sir, I'm too old to learn. Don't call for the stocks. I serve the king, on whose order I was sent to you. If you stock his messenger, you pay no respect and insult my master's dignity as a king as well as his personal honor.*

CORNWALL: *Bring the stocks. Upon my life and honor, he shall sit there till noon.*

REGAN: *Till noon? Till night, my lord, and all night, too!*

130   KENT: Why, madam, if I were your father's dog,
       You should not use me so.

    REGAN: Sir, being his knave, I will.

    CORNWALL: This is a fellow of the self-same colour
       Our sister speaks of. Come, bring away the stocks!
                                 [Stocks brought out]

135   GLOUCESTER: Let me beseech your grace not to do so:
       His fault is much, and the good king his master
       Will cheque him for 't: your purposed low correction
       Is such as basest and contemned'st wretches
       For pilferings and most common trespasses
140   Are punish'd with: the king must take it ill,
       That he's so slightly valued in his messenger,
       Should have him thus restrain'd.

    CORNWALL: I'll answer that.

    REGAN: My sister may receive it much more worse,
145   To have her gentleman abused, assaulted,
       For following her affairs. Put in his legs.
                        [Kent is put in the stocks]
       Come, my good lord, away.

            [Exeunt all but Gloucester and Kent]

    GLOUCESTER: I am sorry for thee, friend; 'tis the duke's pleasure,
       Whose disposition, all the world well knows,
150   Will not be rubb'd nor stopp'd: I'll entreat for thee.

    KENT: Pray, do not, sir: I have watched and travell'd hard;
       Some time I shall sleep out, the rest I'll whistle.
       A good man's fortune may grow out at heels:
       Give you good morrow!

KENT: *Why, madam, you wouldn't treat me like that if I were your father's dog.*

REGAN: *Sir, being his servant, I will.*

CORNWALL: *This is the kind of fellow my sister was speaking of. Come, bring the stocks at once.*

[The stocks are brought]

GLOUCESTER: *Let me beg your Grace not to do this! His fault is great, and the good king his master will rebuke him for it. The shameful punishment you propose for him is used to punish the lowest and most despised villains for thievery and other common transgressions. The king will be angry that you don't honor his messenger and give orders to have him tied up in this manner.*

CORNWALL: *I'll answer to that.*

REGAN: *My sister may take it worse to have her servant abused and assaulted for obeying her orders. Put his legs in.*

[Kent is put in stocks]

Come, my good lord, let's leave.

[All exit except for Gloucester and Kent]

GLOUCESTER: *I'm sorry for you, friend. It's the duke's enjoyment. The whole world knows that his moods cannot be impeded or restrained. I'll plead for you.*

KENT: *Please, don't do that, sir. I've gone without sleep and traveled for long. I'll sleep away some of the time; the rest of the time, I'll whistle. One shouldn't brood over misfortune, since it happens even to good man. Good day to you.*

155   GLOUCESTER: The duke's to blame in this; 'twill be ill taken.

[Exit]

KENT: Good king, that must approve the common saw,
    Thou out of heaven's benediction comest
    To the warm sun!
    Approach, thou beacon to this under globe,
160   That by thy comfortable beams I may
    Peruse this letter! Nothing almost sees miracles
    But misery: I know 'tis from Cordelia,
    Who hath most fortunately been inform'd
    Of my obscured course; and shall find time
165   From this enormous state, seeking to give
    Losses their remedies. All weary and o'erwatch'd,
    Take vantage, heavy eyes, not to behold
    This shameful lodging.
    Fortune, good night: smile once more: turn thy wheel!

[Sleeps]

SCENE III

A wood.

[Enter Edgar]

EDGAR: I heard myself proclaim'd;
    And by the happy hollow of a tree
    Escaped the hunt. No port is free; no place,
    That guard, and most unusual vigilance,
5   Does not attend my taking. Whiles I may 'scape,
    I will preserve myself: and am bethought
    To take the basest and most poorest shape
    That ever penury, in contempt of man,
    Brought near to beast: my face I'll grime with filth;

GLOUCESTER: *The duke's to blame for this! This will be taken badly.*

[Gloucester exits]

KENT: *Good king, who must prove the common proverb true: "You go from better to worse." Come closer to earth, oh moon, so that I may examine this letter by the light of your comforting beams. Almost nobody but the unfortunate can see miracles. I know it's from Cordelia, who, fortunately, has been informed of my disguised appearance. She will find time to set these monstrous conditions right. Oh heavy eyes, fatigued and exhausted from lack of sleep, take this opportunity to sleep and not look at the shameful stocks. Oh fortune, good night. Smile once more, then turn your wheel.*

• STOCKS: laughing stocks

[Kent sleeps]

SCENE III

A wood.

[Edgar enters]

EDGAR: *I heard that I was proclaimed an outlaw and escaped the hunt by hiding in a convenient hollow of a tree. No seaport is free for me; there's no place unguarded where people don't wait to take me prisoner. While I'm trying to escape, I will protect myself. I'm resolved to assume the most simple and primitive disguise which inhuman poverty brought down to the level of a mere beast. I'll smear my face with dirt, wear a cloth around my loins, entangle my hair and bravely face the winds and the*

10   Blanket my loins: elf all my hair in knots;
    And with presented nakedness out-face
    The winds and persecutions of the sky.
    The country gives me proof and precedent
    Of Bedlam beggars, who, with roaring voices,
15   Strike in their numb'd and mortified bare arms
    Pins, wooden pricks, nails, sprigs of rosemary;
    And with this horrible object, from low farms,
    Poor pelting villages, sheep-cotes, and mills,
    Sometime with lunatic bans, sometime with prayers,
20   Enforce their charity. Poor Turlygod! poor Tom!
    That's something yet: Edgar I nothing am.

[Exit]

SCENE IV

Before Gloucester's castle. Kent in the stocks.

[Enter King Lear, Fool, and Gentleman]

KING LEAR: 'Tis strange that they should so depart from home,
    And not send back my messenger.

GENTLEMAN: As I learn'd,
    The night before there was no purpose in them
5   Of this remove.

KENT: Hail to thee, noble master!

KING LEAR: Ha!
    Makest thou this shame thy pastime?

KENT: No, my lord.

10 FOOL: Ha, ha! he wears cruel garters. Horses are tied by the heads,

104

torturous elements with my exposed nakedness. Throughout the country, there are many examples and precedents of mad beggars who, with roaring voices, slam pins, wooden spikes, nails, and rosemary sprigs into their numb and deadened bare arms. With this horrible spectacle, they demand charity from small farms, poverty-stricken villages, sheep cottages, and mills, sometimes with mad curses, sometimes with prayers. Poor beggar. Poor Tom. There's that much left for me. As Edgar, I am nothing at all.

[Edgar exits]

talking to himself ( ) about his plan to escape → disguise himself.

SCENE IV

Before Gloucester's castle. Kent [disguised] in stocks.

[Lear, Fool, and Gentleman enter]

KING LEAR: It's strange that they should leave home like that and not send back my messenger.

GENTLEMAN: I've heard that, last night, they had no plans for leaving their residence.

KENT: Greetings to you, noble master.

KING LEAR: Ha! Are you undergoing this humiliation for fun?

KENT: No, my lord.

FOOL: Ha, ha! He's wearing stocks! Horses are tied up by their heads, dogs and bears by the neck, monkeys by the loins, and men by the legs: when a man's over-lusty at legs, then he wears wooden nether-stocks.

15 KING LEAR: What's he that hath so much thy place mistook
To set thee here?

KENT: It is both he and she;
Your son and daughter.

KING LEAR: No.

KENT: Yes.

20 KING LEAR: No, I say.

KENT: I say, yea.

KING LEAR: No, no, they would not.

KENT: Yes, they have.

KING LEAR: By Jupiter, I swear, no.

25 KENT: By Juno, I swear, ay.

KING LEAR: They durst not do't;
They could not, would not do't; 'tis worse than murder,
To do upon respect such violent outrage:
Resolve me, with all modest haste, which way
30 Thou mightst deserve, or they impose, this usage,
Coming from us.

KENT: My lord, when at their home
I did commend your highness' letters to them,

dogs and bears by their necks, monkeys by their waists, and men by their legs. When a man has run away from service, he must wear wooden stockings.

KING LEAR: Who has ignored your position as the king's messenger and placed you here in stocks?

KENT: It's both her and him; your son-in-law and your daughter.

KING LEAR: No.

KENT: Yes.

KING LEAR: No, I say!

KENT: I say, yes!

KING LEAR: No, no, they wouldn't!

KENT: Yes, they have!

KING LEAR: By Jupiter, I swear no!

KENT: By Juno, I swear yes!

KING LEAR: They wouldn't dare to do it! They couldn't, they wouldn't do it! It's worse than murder to commit such a violent insult against the king through his messenger. Inform me, quickly but reasonably, why you might deserve—or why they would impose—this treatment on my messenger.

k. L. is naive to Cornelia and her inventions

KENT: My lord, when I was at their home and delivered your letter to them, I was kneeling dutifully when a sweaty courier arrived. Hot

Ere I was risen from the place that show'd
35 My duty kneeling, came there a reeking post,
    Stew'd in his haste, half breathless, panting forth
    From Goneril his mistress salutations;
    Deliver'd letters, spite of intermission,
    Which presently they read: on whose contents,
40 They summon'd up their meiny, straight took horse;
    Commanded me to follow, and attend
    The leisure of their answer; gave me cold looks:
    And meeting here the other messenger,
    Whose welcome, I perceived, had poison'd mine,—
45 Being the very fellow that of late
    Display'd so saucily against your highness,—
    Having more man than wit about me, drew:
    He raised the house with loud and coward cries.
    Your son and daughter found this trespass worth
50 The shame which here it suffers.

Fool: Winter's not gone yet, if the wild-geese fly that way.
            Fathers that wear rags
                Do make their children blind;
            But fathers that bear bags
55   Shall see their children kind.
            Fortune, that arrant whore,
                Ne'er turns the key to the poor.
    But, for all this, thou shalt have as many dolours for thy daugh-
    ters as thou canst tell in a year.

60 King Lear: O, how this mother swells up toward my heart!
    Hysterica passio, down, thou climbing sorrow,
    Thy element's below! Where is this daughter?

Kent: With the earl, sir, here within.

King Lear: Follow me not;
65   Stay here.   [Exit]

Gentleman: Made you no more offence but what you speak of?

from running and nearly breathless, he stammered salutations from his mistress Goneril and delivered a letter, careless of interrupting me. They opened it immediately, and, on reading its contents, called together their household, instantly mounted their horses, and commanded me to follow them and to await an answer at their leisure. They gave me cold looks! When I met the other messenger here, whose welcome, I felt, had ruined mine, and recognized him as the fellow who had recently behaved so insolently against your highness, I felt more courage than common sense and drew my sword. He alarmed the house with loud and cowardly screams. Your son-in-law and your daughter thought this transgression deserved the humiliation that I now suffer.

FOOL: *Winter isn't over yet, if the wild geese are still flying around.*
Fathers who wear rags make their children blind, but
fathers who have money will have grateful children.
Fortune, that shameless whore, never opens the door
for the poor!
But for all this, you'll receive more pain from your daughters than you can handle in one year.

} predicting + exposing his daughter + her ungrateful d.

KING LEAR: *Oh, how this choking sensation strangles my throat! Hysteria, you disease that brings rising sorrow, stay in your proper place! Where is this daughter?*

doesn't say my

KENT: *With the Earl, sir, inside.*

KING LEAR: *Don't follow me. Stay here.*

[Lear exits]

GENTLEMAN: *Did you commit no other offense than the one you have described?*

KENT: None.
How chance the king comes with so small a train?

FOOL: And thou hadst been set i' the stocks for that question, thou
70   hadst well deserved it.

KENT: Why, fool?

FOOL: We'll set thee to school to an ant, to teach thee there's no
labouring i' the winter. All that follow their noses are led by
their eyes but blind men; and there's not a nose among twenty
75   but can smell him that's stinking. Let go thy hold when a great
wheel runs down a hill, lest it break thy neck with following it:
but the great one that goes up the hill, let him draw thee after.
When a wise man gives thee better counsel, give me mine again:
I would have none but knaves follow it, since a fool gives it.
80   That sir which serves and seeks for gain,
                 And follows but for form,
              Will pack when it begins to rain,
                 And leave thee in the storm,
              But I will tarry; the fool will stay,
85   And let the wise man fly:
              The knave turns fool that runs away;
                 The fool no knave, perdy.

KENT: Where learned you this, fool?

FOOL: Not i' the stocks, fool.

[Re-enter King Lear with Gloucester]

90   KING LEAR: Deny to speak with me? They are sick? they are weary?
They have travell'd all the night? Mere fetches;
The images of revolt and flying off.
Fetch me a better answer.

KENT: None. Why does the king come with so few followers?

FOOL: If you had been put in stocks for that question, you would have deserved it.

KENT: Why, Fool?

FOOL: The wise ant knows that there are no profits to be gained in the winter! All who follow their noses are led by their eyes, except for the blind, and there's not one nose among twenty of them that can't smell a loser. Loosen your grip when a big wheel runs down a hill, or you'll break your neck trying to keep up with it, but when the big wheel goes uphill, let it drag you along. When a wise man gives you better advice, give mine back! I only want scoundrels to follow it, because it was given by a fool.

> The knight who serves for the sake of gain and follows without loyalty will depart when it begins to rain and leave you in the storm. But I will stay, the fool will stay, and let the wiser men leave. The scoundrel turns into a fool when he runs away. The fool is certainly no scoundrel.

insight on loyalty

KENT: Where did you learn this, Fool?

FOOL: Not in the stocks, you fool.

[Lear enters with Gloucester]

KING LEAR: They refuse to speak to me? They are sick? They are tired? They have traveled all night? Merely excuses! Signs of revolt and desertion! Give me a better answer!

king lear is beginning to catch on.

111

GLOUCESTER: My dear lord,

95   You know the fiery quality of the duke;
     How unremoveable and fix'd he is
     In his own course.

KING LEAR: Vengeance! plague! death! confusion!
     Fiery? what quality? Why, Gloucester, Gloucester,
100   I'd speak with the Duke of Cornwall and his wife.

GLOUCESTER: Well, my good lord, I have inform'd them so.

KING LEAR: Inform'd them! Dost thou understand me, man?

GLOUCESTER: Ay, my good lord.

KING LEAR: The king would speak with Cornwall; the dear father
105   Would with his daughter speak, commands her service:
     Are they inform'd of this? My breath and blood!
     Fiery? the fiery duke? Tell the hot duke that—
     No, but not yet: may be he is not well:
     Infirmity doth still neglect all office
110   Whereto our health is bound; we are not ourselves
     When nature, being oppress'd, commands the mind
     To suffer with the body: I'll forbear;
     And am fall'n out with my more headier will,
     To take the indisposed and sickly fit
115   For the sound man. Death on my state! wherefore
     [Looking on Kent]
     Should he sit here? This act persuades me
     That this remotion of the duke and her
     Is practise only. Give me my servant forth.
     Go tell the duke and's wife I'd speak with them,
120   Now, presently: bid them come forth and hear me,
     Or at their chamber-door I'll beat the drum
     Till it cry sleep to death.

GLOUCESTER: I would have all well betwixt you. *[Exit]*

112

GLOUCESTER: *My dear lord, you know the fiery nature of the duke, how stubborn and resolute he is in his actions.*

KING LEAR: *Vengeance! Plague! Death! Confusion. "Fiery"? What "nature"? Gloucester, Gloucester, I want to speak with the Duke of Cornwall and his wife!*

GLOUCESTER: *Well, my good lord, I have informed them of it.*

KING LEAR: *Informed them? Do you understand me, man?*

GLOUCESTER: *Yes, my good lord.*

KING LEAR: *The king wants to speak to Cornwall. The king wants to speak to his daughter, demands her obedience. Have they been "informed" of this? My breath and blood! "Fiery"? The "fiery" duke? Tell the hot duke that—no, not yet. Perhaps he isn't well. When in illness, we always neglect the duties we are bound to honor in health. We're not ourselves when our compromised health causes the mind to suffer along with the body. I'll restrain myself and reject my headstrong impulse to treat an ailing and sickly man as if he was a healthy man. [Looking on Kent] Death to my royal power! Why should he sit here? This act persuades me that the aloofness of her and the duke is only trickery. Give my servant back! Go tell the duke and his wife that I want to speak with them. Now, immediately! Tell them to come here and listen to me, or I'll pound at their bedroom-door until the noise makes sleep impossible.*

- grasping onto the power
+
auth she was given + is working to take
from him.

GLOUCESTER: *I wish everything was well between you.* [Exit]

113

KING LEAR: O me, my heart, my rising heart! but, down!

125   FOOL: Cry to it, nuncle, as the cockney did to the eels when she put
'em i' the paste alive; she knapped 'em o' the coxcombs with
a stick, and cried "Down, wantons, down!" 'Twas her brother
that, in pure kindness to his horse, buttered his hay.

[Enter Cornwall, Regan, Gloucester, and Servants]

KING LEAR: Good morrow to you both.

130   CORNWALL: Hail to your grace!   *[Kent is set at liberty]*

REGAN: I am glad to see your highness.

KING LEAR: Regan, I think you are; I know what reason
I have to think so: if thou shouldst not be glad,
I would divorce me from thy mother's tomb,
135   Sepulchring an adultress. *[To Kent]* O, are you free?
Some other time for that. Beloved Regan,
Thy sister's naught: O Regan, she hath tied
Sharp-tooth'd unkindness, like a vulture, here:
[Points to his heart]
I can scarce speak to thee; thou'lt not believe
140   With how depraved a quality—O Regan!

REGAN: I pray you, sir, take patience: I have hope.
You less know how to value her desert
Than she to scant her duty.

KING LEAR: Say, how is that?

KING LEAR: *Oh me, my heart, my rising heart! Stay down!*

FOOL: *Yell at it, my uncle, as the affected woman did to the eels when she put them into the pie alive. She cracked them over the head with a stick and cried, "Down, you lively creatures, down!" It was her brother who, out of pure kindness, put butter on his hay.*

[Gloucester reenters with Cornwall, Regan, and Servants]

KING LEAR: *Good morning to you both.*

CORNWALL: *Hail to your Grace.* [Kent is set at liberty]

REGAN: *I am glad to see your highness.*

KING LEAR: *Regan, I'm sure you are. I know why I have to think so: If you weren't glad, I would renounce your mother's grave, certain that it bears the body of an adulteress.* [To Kent] *Oh, are you free? We'll deal with that some other time. Beloved Regan, your sister is wicked. Oh, Regan, she has attacked my heart, like a vulture, with sharp-toothed unkindness.* [He points to his heart] *I can barely speak to you. You would not believe the corrupted manner in which—oh Regan.*

REGAN: *I beg you, sir, please control yourself. I rather hope that you aren't valuing her merit enough than that she is neglecting her duty.*

I hope you aren't valuing her praise enough that she is not doing what she is given to do.

KING LEAR: *Tell me, how can that be?*

145 REGAN: I cannot think my sister in the least
Would fail her obligation: if, sir, perchance
She have restrain'd the riots of your followers,
'Tis on such ground, and to such wholesome end,
As clears her from all blame.

150 KING LEAR: My curses on her!

REGAN: O, sir, you are old.
Nature in you stands on the very verge
Of her confine: you should be ruled and led
By some discretion, that discerns your state
155 Better than you yourself. Therefore, I pray you,
That to our sister you do make return;
Say you have wrong'd her, sir.

KING LEAR: Ask her forgiveness?
Do you but mark how this becomes the house:
160 [Kneeling] 'Dear daughter, I confess that I am old;
Age is unnecessary: on my knees I beg
That you'll vouchsafe me raiment, bed, and food.'

REGAN: Good sir, no more; these are unsightly tricks:
Return you to my sister.

165 KING LEAR: [Rising]   Never, Regan:
She hath abated me of half my train;
Look'd black upon me; struck me with her tongue,
Most serpent-like, upon the very heart:
All the stored vengeances of heaven fall
170 On her ingrateful top! Strike her young bones,
You taking airs, with lameness!

CORNWALL: Fie, sir, fie!

KING LEAR: You nimble lightnings, dart your blinding flames
Into her scornful eyes! Infect her beauty,
175 You fen-suck'd fogs, drawn by the powerful sun,
To fall and blast her pride!

116

REGAN: I cannot believe that my sister would neglect her obligations in the least. If, sir, she has perhaps restrained the riots of your followers, it is for good reasons and with honorable intentions that would clear her from all blame.

→ the only honorable thing she could do is reign in riots rather than instigate havoc.

KING LEAR: My curses on her!

REGAN: Oh, sir, you are old. Your natural life is reaching its limits. You should be ruled and led by someone able to judge your condition better than yourself. Therefore, I beg you to return to our sister. Tell her that you've wronged her, sir.

KING LEAR: Ask her forgiveness? Do you think this accords with the decorum fit for a royal family? [Lear kneels] "Dear daughter, I confess that I am old. Old people are unnecessary. On my knees I beg that you'll give me clothes, a bed, and food."

REGAN: Good sir, no more of this. These are ugly tricks. Return to my sister!

Reagan advises him to forgive her + ask her to forgive him

KING LEAR: [Rising] Never, Regan! She has taken away half of my following, looked at me angrily, and struck my very heart with her venomous tongue, like a serpent. May the concentrated vengeance of heaven fall on her ungrateful head! Strike her unborn infant with lameness, oh infectious air!

His guilt of mistake + misfortune is shown in anger towards her.

CORNWALL: Come on now, sir, come on!

KING LEAR: Oh skillful lightning, shoot your blinding flames into her scornful eyes! Infect her beauty, you fogs rising from the swamps, drawn out by the powerful sun, strike her and shatter her pride!

REGAN: O the blest gods! so will you wish on me,
    When the rash mood is on.

KING LEAR: No, Regan, thou shalt never have my curse:
180   Thy tender-hefted nature shall not give
    Thee o'er to harshness: her eyes are fierce; but thine
    Do comfort and not burn. 'Tis not in thee
    To grudge my pleasures, to cut off my train,
    To bandy hasty words, to scant my sizes,
185   And in conclusion to oppose the bolt
    Against my coming in: thou better know'st
    The offices of nature, bond of childhood,
    Effects of courtesy, dues of gratitude;
    Thy half o' the kingdom hast thou not forgot,
190   Wherein I thee endow'd.

REGAN: Good sir, to the purpose.

KING LEAR: Who put my man i' the stocks?   [Tucket within]

CORNWALL: What trumpet's that?

REGAN: I know't, my sister's: this approves her letter,
195   That she would soon be here.

[Enter Oswald]
            Is your lady come?

KING LEAR: This is a slave, whose easy-borrow'd pride
    Dwells in the fickle grace of her he follows.
    Out, varlet, from my sight!

200 CORNWALL: What means your grace?

KING LEAR: Who stock'd my servant? Regan, I have good hope
    Thou didst not know on't. Who comes here? O heavens,

REGAN: Oh, the blessed gods! That's what you'll wish on me, when a rash mood strikes you.

KING LEAR: No, Regan. I will never curse you. Your loving nature would never turn to harshness. Her eyes are fierce, but yours comfort and don't burn. It's not in your nature to spoil my pleasures, to reduce my following, to exchange unfriendly words, to restrict my allowance, and, finally, to lock me out. You are aware of your natural duties, the bond between parent and child, proper behavior, and appropriate gratitude. You have not forgotten about your half of the kingdom that I gave to you.

REGAN: Good sir, let's get to the point!

KING LEAR: Who put my servant in stocks? [A trumpet sounds]

CORNWALL: Whose trumpet is this?

REGAN: I know it. It's my sister's. This confirms her letter saying that she would soon be here.

[Oswald enters]
Has your lady arrived?

KING LEAR: This is the slave whose cheap pride depends on the uncertain favor of his mistress. Out, villain, out of my sight!

CORNWALL: What does your Grace mean?

KING LEAR: Who put my servant in stocks? Regan, I hope you did not know about it. Who comes here?

[Enter Goneril]
    If you do love old men, if your sweet sway
    Allow obedience, if yourselves are old,
205   Make it your cause; send down, and take my part!
    [To Goneril] Art not ashamed to look upon this beard?
    O Regan, wilt thou take her by the hand?

GONERIL: Why not by the hand, sir? How have I offended?
    All's not offence that indiscretion finds
210   And dotage terms so.

KING LEAR: O sides, you are too tough;
    Will you yet hold? How came my man i' the stocks?

CORNWALL: I set him there, sir: but his own disorders
    Deserved much less advancement.

215 KING LEAR: You! did you?

REGAN: I pray you, father, being weak, seem so.
    If, till the expiration of your month,
    You will return and sojourn with my sister,
    Dismissing half your train, come then to me:
220   I am now from home, and out of that provision
    Which shall be needful for your entertainment.

KING LEAR: Return to her, and fifty men dismiss'd?
    No, rather I abjure all roofs, and choose
    To wage against the enmity o' the air;
225   To be a comrade with the wolf and owl,—
    Necessity's sharp pinch! Return with her?
    Why, the hot-blooded France, that dowerless took
    Our youngest born, I could as well be brought
    To knee his throne, and, squire-like; pension beg
230   To keep base life afoot. Return with her?
    Persuade me rather to be slave and sumpter
    To this detested groom.   *[Pointing at Oswald]*

120

[Goneril enters]

Oh heavenly gods, if you love old men, if your controlling influence approves of obedience, if you're old yourselves, make this your cause. Come down and take my side. [To Goneril] Are you not ashamed to look at this beard? Oh, Regan, will you take her hand?

GONERIL: Why not my hand, sir? How have I offended you? Not everything is an offense that is called so by thoughtlessness and old age.

KING LEAR: Oh, my heart! You are tough! Will you not break yet? Why is my man in stocks?

CORNWALL: I put him there, sir, although his disobedience deserved far worse punishment.

KING LEAR: You! Did you?

REGAN: I beg you, father, you are weak. Don't pretend to be otherwise. If you will return to my sister and reside with her until the end of the month and discharge half of your following, you can then come and stay with me. Right now, I'm away from home and unable to provide whatever is necessary for your maintenance.

His anger of distrust + backstabbing is undermined by his daughters as "adage".

KING LEAR: Return to her and dismiss fifty men? No, I'd rather abandon any residence, battle the unfriendly elements, and befriend wolves and owls. Cruel fate! Return to her? I might as well kneel at the throne of the king of France, who took our youngest daughter without dowry, and, like a squire, beg for money to keep up a lowly existence. Return to her? You can persuade me more easily to be this servant's slave and packhorse! [Pointing at Oswald]

Exaggeration of the extent of his anger.

121

GONERIL: At your choice, sir.

KING LEAR: I prithee, daughter, do not make me mad:
235   I will not trouble thee, my child; farewell:
         We'll no more meet, no more see one another:
         But yet thou art my flesh, my blood, my daughter;
         Or rather a disease that's in my flesh,
         Which I must needs call mine: thou art a boil,
240   A plague-sore, an embossed carbuncle,
         In my corrupted blood. But I'll not chide thee;
         Let shame come when it will, I do not call it:
         I do not bid the thunder-bearer shoot,
         Nor tell tales of thee to high-judging Jove:
245   Mend when thou canst; be better at thy leisure:
         I can be patient; I can stay with Regan,
         I and my hundred knights.

REGAN: Not altogether so:
         I look'd not for you yet, nor am provided
250   For your fit welcome. Give ear, sir, to my sister;
         For those that mingle reason with your passion
         Must be content to think you old, and so—
         But she knows what she does.

KING LEAR: Is this well spoken?

255 REGAN: I dare avouch it, sir: what, fifty followers?
         Is it not well? What should you need of more?
         Yea, or so many, sith that both charge and danger
         Speak 'gainst so great a number? How, in one house,
         Should many people, under two commands,
260   Hold amity? 'Tis hard; almost impossible.

GONERIL: Why might not you, my lord, receive attendance
         From those that she calls servants or from mine?

GENERIL: *If you wish, sir.*

KING LEAR: *I beg you, daughter. Don't make me mad! I won't trouble you, my child. Goodbye. We'll never meet again nor see each other again. Still, you are my flesh and blood, my daughter. Or, rather, a disease within my body that I must acknowledge. You're a boil, a plague-sore, a swollen tumor in my diseased blood! But I won't scold you. Let shame come over you at its own pace—I won't summon it. I do not ask Jupiter to send his thunderbolts nor tell tales about you to Jove, who judges from above. Improve as soon as you can, be better at your own leisure. I can be patient. I can stay with Regan; I and my hundred knights.*

REGAN: *Not quite. I was not expecting you yet, nor am I prepared to welcome you properly. Listen to my sister, sir. Anyone who applies good judgment to your passionate words must conclude that you're old, and so—but she knows what she's doing.*

KING LEAR: *Is that what you mean?*

REGAN: *I vouch for it, sir. Fifty followers? Is that not good enough? What need should you have for more? Yes, or so many, since both the expenses and the danger for riotous behavior speak against such a big number. How can this many people under two different commands live peacefully in one house? It's hard, almost impossible.*

GONERIL: *Why couldn't you, my lord, be attended by her servants, or by mine?*

123

REGAN: Why not, my lord? If then they chanced to slack you,
    We could control them. If you will come to me,—
265   For now I spy a danger,—I entreat you
    To bring but five and twenty: to no more
    Will I give place or notice.

KING LEAR: I gave you all—

REGAN: And in good time you gave it.

270 KING LEAR: Made you my guardians, my depositaries;
    But kept a reservation to be follow'd
    With such a number. What, must I come to you
    With five and twenty, Regan? said you so?

REGAN: And speak't again, my lord; no more with me.

275 KING LEAR: Those wicked creatures yet do look well-favour'd,
    When others are more wicked: not being the worst
    Stands in some rank of praise. *[To Goneril]* I'll go with thee:
    Thy fifty yet doth double five and twenty,
    And thou art twice her love.

280 GONERIL: Hear me, my lord;
    What need you five and twenty, ten, or five,
    To follow in a house where twice so many
    Have a command to tend you?

REGAN: What need one?

285 KING LEAR: O, reason not the need: our basest beggars
    Are in the poorest thing superfluous:
    Allow not nature more than nature needs,
    Man's life's as cheap as beast's: thou art a lady;
    If only to go warm were gorgeous,
290   Why, nature needs not what thou gorgeous wear'st,

REGAN: *Why not, my lord? Then, if they happened to neglect their duties toward you, we could discipline them. If you stay with me, since now I perceive a dangerous situation, I'm asking you to bring only twenty-five followers. I will not provide room or recognition to more of your men.*

Reagan is also working to passively take his power away

KING LEAR: *I gave you everything!*

his daughters make him feel he is crazy.

REGAN: *And took your time till you gave it.*

KING LEAR: *Made you my protectors, my trustees, but kept the right to keep a following of such a number. What, must I come to you with twenty-five, Regan? Is that what you said?*

REGAN: *And I say it again, my lord. No more with me.*

KING LEAR: *Some wicked creatures still look good when you compare them to others who are more wicked. Not being the worst deserves some kind of reward.* [To Goneril] *I'll come with you. Your fifty is still double the number of her twenty-five, so you offer twice her love.*

He has a warped sense of love + they see that.

GONERIL: *Hear me, my lord. What do you need twenty-five, ten, or five men to be your followers when you're in a house where twice that many are ordered to serve you?*

manipulative

REGAN: *Why need one?*

KING LEAR: *Don't argue about "need." poorest beggars have some miserable possessions they don't "need." If you don't allow nature to have more than nature needs, then man's life becomes as worthless as that of a beast. You are a lady. If staying warm*

Which scarcely keeps thee warm. But, for true need,—
You heavens, give me that patience, patience I need!
You see me here, you gods, a poor old man,
As full of grief as age; wretched in both!
295   If it be you that stir these daughters' hearts
Against their father, fool me not so much
To bear it tamely; touch me with noble anger,
And let not women's weapons, water-drops,
Stain my man's cheeks! No, you unnatural hags,
300   I will have such revenges on you both,
That all the world shall—I will do such things,—
What they are, yet I know not: but they shall be
The terrors of the earth. You think I'll weep
No, I'll not weep:
305   I have full cause of weeping; but this heart
Shall break into a hundred thousand flaws,
Or ere I'll weep. O fool, I shall go mad!

[Exeunt King Lear, Gloucester, Kent, and Fool]

CORNWALL: Let us withdraw; 'twill be a storm.

[Storm and tempest]

REGAN: This house is little: the old man and his people
310   Cannot be well bestow'd.

GONERIL: 'Tis his own blame; hath put himself from rest,
And must needs taste his folly.

REGAN: For his particular, I'll receive him gladly,
But not one follower.

315 GONERIL: So am I purposed.
Where is my lord of Gloucester?

CORNWALL: Follow'd the old man forth: he is return'd.

was the only purpose of fashion, then you wouldn't need the fashionable clothes you wear, which barely keep you warm. But for true need,—oh, heavens, give me the patience that I need. You see me here, oh gods, a poor old man, with as much grief as age, miserable in both respects. If you provoke my daughter's hearts against their father, don't make me such a fool as to take it calmly. Fill me with noble anger, and let no woman's weapons, tears, run down my cheeks! No, you unnatural witches! I will do things in revenge to show all the world—I will do things— exactly what, I don't know yet, but it'll be terrifying! You think I'll cry. No, I won't cry. I have enough reason for crying, but this heart shall break into a hundred thousand fragments before I cry. Oh, Fool, I will go mad!

[Lear, Gloucester, Kent, and Fool exit]

CORNWALL: Let's go inside; a storm is coming!
[A storm and tempest rage]

REGAN: This house is small. The old man and his followers cannot be adequately lodged.

GONERIL: It's his own fault. He has disturbed his own peace of mind and must now suffer for his foolishness.

REGAN: As far as he himself is concerned, I'll receive him gladly, but not one follower.

GONERIL: That is my intention, too. Where is my lord of Gloucester?

CORNWALL: Followed the old man. He's back.

Both on the same page against Lear.

127

[Re-enter Gloucester]

GLOUCESTER: The king is in high rage.

CORNWALL: Whither is he going?

320 GLOUCESTER: He calls to horse; but will I know not whither.

CORNWALL: 'Tis best to give him way; he leads himself.

GONERIL: My lord, entreat him by no means to stay.

GLOUCESTER: Alack, the night comes on, and the bleak winds
        Do sorely ruffle; for many miles a bout
325   There's scarce a bush.

REGAN: O, sir, to wilful men,
        The injuries that they themselves procure
        Must be their schoolmasters. Shut up your doors:
        He is attended with a desperate train;
330   And what they may incense him to, being apt
        To have his ear abused, wisdom bids fear.

CORNWALL: Shut up your doors, my lord; 'tis a wild night:
        My Regan counsels well; come out o' the storm.

                              [Exeunt]

[Gloucester reenters]

GLOUCESTER: *The king is enraged.*

CORNWALL: *Where is he going?*

GLOUCESTER: *He's calling for his horses, but I don't know where he's going?*

CORNWALL: *It's best to let him have his way.* He is his own master.

GONERIL: *My lord, by no means ask him to stay!*

GLOUCESTER: *Alas, it's almost night, and the bleak winds rage angrily. There's barely a bush for many miles.*

REGAN: *Oh, sir, willful men must learn from the injuries they bring on themselves. Shut your doors! He is attended by a reckless bunch! Common sense tells us to fear whatever they may incite him to do. He is prone to being deceived.*

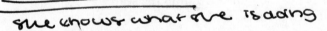
she knows what she is doing

CORNWALL: *Lock your doors, my lord; it's a wild night. My Regan is right. Come out of the storm.*

[All exit]

ACT III

SCENE I

A heath.

[Storm still. Enter Kent and a Gentleman, meeting]

KENT: Who's there, besides foul weather?

GENTLEMAN: One minded like the weather, most unquietly.

KENT: I know you. Where's the king?

GENTLEMAN: Contending with the fretful element:
5 Bids the winds blow the earth into the sea,
  Or swell the curled water 'bove the main,
  That things might change or cease; tears his white hair,
  Which the impetuous blasts, with eyeless rage,
  Catch in their fury, and make nothing of;
10 Strives in his little world of man to out-scorn
  The to-and-fro-conflicting wind and rain.
  This night, wherein the cub-drawn bear would couch,
  The lion and the belly-pinched wolf
  Keep their fur dry, unbonneted he runs,
15 And bids what will take all.

  KENT: But who is with him?

ACT III

SCENE I

A heath near Gloucester's castle.

[The storm still rages. Kent and a Gentleman meet]

KENT: *Who's there, besides foul weather?*

GENTLEMAN: *Someone disturbed, like the storm.*

KENT: *I know you. Where's the king?*

Does the storm represent the storm raging w/ his daughters

GENTLEMAN: *Struggling with the turbulent elements. He asks the wind to blow the earth into the sea or raise the waves above the mainland, to bring about chaos or destruction. He tears his white hair, which rushing winds, in blind rage, catch in their fury and blow about disrespectfully. He attempts to out-storm the raging wind and rain within his little human world. On this night, when even the hungry bear stays in its lair, when the lion and the starving wolf try to keep their fur dry, he runs about unprotected and cries for the destruction of the world.*

old.

the king is in "blind rage" he is mad and cannot think w/ one. reason why — when he is given a reason to accept love he will.

KENT: *But who is with him?*

GENTLEMAN: None but the fool; who labours to out-jest
    His heart-struck injuries.

KENT: Sir, I do know you;
20   And dare, upon the warrant of my note,
    Commend a dear thing to you. There is division,
    Although as yet the face of it be cover'd
    With mutual cunning, 'twixt Albany and Cornwall;
    Who have—as who have not, that their great stars
25   Throned and set high?—servants, who seem no less,
    Which are to France the spies and speculations
    Intelligent of our state; what hath been seen,
    Either in snuffs and packings of the dukes,
    Or the hard rein which both of them have borne
30   Against the old kind king; or something deeper,
    Whereof perchance these are but furnishings;
    But, true it is, from France there comes a power
    Into this scatter'd kingdom; who already,
    Wise in our negligence, have secret feet
35   In some of our best ports, and are at point
    To show their open banner. Now to you:
    If on my credit you dare build so far
    To make your speed to Dover, you shall find
    Some that will thank you, making just report
40   Of how unnatural and bemadding sorrow
    The king hath cause to plain.
    I am a gentleman of blood and breeding;
    And, from some knowledge and assurance, offer
    This office to you.

45 GENTLEMAN: I will talk further with you.

KENT: No, do not.
    For confirmation that I am much more
    Than my out-wall, open this purse, and take
    What it contains. If you shall see Cordelia,—
50   As fear not but you shall,—show her this ring;

GENTLEMAN: *Nobody but the fool, who tries to relieve the king's <u>emotional injuries</u> with his jokes.*

KENT: Sir, I do know you, and I dare, due to my impression of you, to entrust you with an important matter. There is a conflict between Albany and Cornwall, although, as of yet, it is still hidden by their craftiness. They, like all who are powerful, have servants. That's what they seem to be. They are secret observers who furnish intelligence about our kingdom to the king of France. They report about the quarrels and plots of the dukes, or the harsh treatment both of them have given to the old king, or something more profound that lies beneath these superficial issues. But the fact is that an army from France is coming into this divided kingdom. Profiting from our negligence, they have already secretly entered our best seaports and are about to reveal their presence. Now, as for you, if you trust me enough to hurry to Dover, you will meet some people who will thank you for an accurate report of the unnatural and maddening affliction the king must suffer from. I am a gentleman of noble birth and good breeding, and, based on confirmed intelligence, I offer this assignment to you.

GENTLEMAN: I'll talk more with you.

KENT: No, don't. To assure you that I am more than what my outward appearance suggests, I want you to open this purse and take what's inside. If you see Cordelia, and be assured that you will, show her this ring, and she will tell you who your companion

And she will tell you who your fellow is
That yet you do not know. Fie on this storm!
I will go seek the king.

GENTLEMAN: Give me your hand: have you no more to say?

55   KENT: Few words, but, to effect, more than all yet;
That, when we have found the king,—in which your pain
That way, I'll this,—he that first lights on him
Holla the other.   *[Exeunt severally]*

SCENE II

Another part of the heath. Storm still.

[Enter King Lear and Fool]

KING LEAR: Blow, winds, and crack your cheeks! rage! blow!
You cataracts and hurricanoes, spout
Till you have drench'd our steeples, drown'd the cocks!
You sulphurous and thought-executing fires,
5   Vaunt-couriers to oak-cleaving thunderbolts,
Singe my white head! And thou, all-shaking thunder,
Smite flat the thick rotundity o' the world!
Crack nature's moulds, an germens spill at once,
That make ingrateful man!

10   FOOL: O nuncle, court holy-water in a dry house is better than this
rain-water out o' door. Good nuncle, in, and ask thy daughters'
blessing: here's a night pities neither wise man nor fool.

134

is who is, as of yet, unknown to you. Damn this storm! I'll go find
the king.

GENTLEMAN: Give me your hand. Don't you have anything else to say?

KENT: Only a few words, but in importance, they are more profound than
anything I've said so far. When we have found the king—your search
will lead you this way and mine that way—let whoever finds him
first alert the other.

[They exit separately]

SCENE II

Another part of the heath. Storm continues.

[Lear and Fool enter]

KING LEAR: Blow, winds, and crack your cheeks! Rage! Blow! You cataracts and waterspouts, spew till you have drenched our church tow-
ers and drowned the weathercocks! You fiery, fast flashes, forerun-
ners of the tree-splitting thunderbolts, scorch my white head! And
you, shattering thunder, flatten the round earth, crack the world's
natural shape, and immediately destroy all seeds from which men
are created!

*The king has lost control so turns mad as a response to
betrayal + takes control of everything: storm*

FOOL: Oh, my uncle, nice words inside a house that is dry are
better than being soaked in this rain outside. Good, uncle, go and
ask your daughters for a blessing. This night pities neither the wise
man nor the fool.

KING LEAR: Rumble thy bellyful! Spit, fire! spout, rain!
    Nor rain, wind, thunder, fire, are my daughters:
15   I tax not you, you elements, with unkindness;
    I never gave you kingdom, call'd you children,
    You owe me no subscription: then let fall
    Your horrible pleasure: here I stand, your slave,
    A poor, infirm, weak, and despised old man:
20   But yet I call you servile ministers,
    That have with two pernicious daughters join'd
    Your high engender'd battles 'gainst a head
    So old and white as this. O! O! 'tis foul!

FOOL: He that has a house to put's head in has a good head-piece.
25   The cod-piece that will house
          Before the head has any,
        The head and he shall louse;
          So beggars marry many.
        The man that makes his toe
30   What he his heart should make
        Shall of a corn cry woe,
          And turn his sleep to wake.
For there was never yet fair woman but she made mouths in a glass.

35 KING LEAR: No, I will be the pattern of all patience;
    I will say nothing.

[Enter Kent]

KENT: Who's there?

FOOL: Marry, here's grace and a cod-piece; that's a wise man and a fool.

40 KENT: Alas, sir, are you here? things that love night
    Love not such nights as these; the wrathful skies
    Gallow the very wanderers of the dark,

KING LEAR: *Rumble as if your belly were full! Spit, fire! Spout, rain! Neither rain, wind, thunder, or fire are my daughters. I don't accuse you elements of unkindness. I never gave you my kingdom, called you my children. You don't owe me your allegiance. Go ahead; indulge in your horrible enjoyment. Here I stand, your slave, a poor, infirm, weak, and despised old man. Yet, I call you heavenly slaves, because you have joined your heavenly armies with two wicked daughters against a head so old and white as this one Oh, oh, it is awful!*

FOOL: *Whoever has a house to put his head in, has a brain.*
       He who engages in sexual intercourse before he can
       afford to keep a house will end up as a beggar. The
       man who kicks away what he should love will feel so
       much pain in his toe that he is unable to sleep.
There has never been a beautiful woman who didn't practice her facial expressions in a mirror.

KING LEAR: *No, I will be an example of patience. I won't say anything!*

[Kent enters in disguise]

KENT: *Who's there?*

FOOL: *Here's someone graceful and someone indecent—a wise man and a fool.*

KENT: *Alas, sir, are you here? Even things that thrive at night don't enjoy nights like these. The angry sky frightens even the creatures that roam at night and makes them stay inside their caves. Since*

go inside king.

And make them keep their caves: since I was man,
Such sheets of fire, such bursts of horrid thunder,
45 Such groans of roaring wind and rain, I never
Remember to have heard: man's nature cannot carry
The affliction nor the fear.

KING LEAR: Let the great gods,
That keep this dreadful pother o'er our heads,
50 Find out their enemies now. Tremble, thou wretch,
That hast within thee undivulged crimes,
Unwhipp'd of justice: hide thee, thou bloody hand;
Thou perjured, and thou simular man of virtue
That art incestuous: caitiff, to pieces shake,
55 That under covert and convenient seeming
Hast practised on man's life: close pent-up guilts,
Rive your concealing continents, and cry
These dreadful summoners grace. I am a man
More sinn'd against than sinning.

60 KENT: Alack, bare-headed!
Gracious my lord, hard by here is a hovel;
Some friendship will it lend you 'gainst the tempest:
Repose you there; while I to this hard house—
More harder than the stones whereof 'tis raised;
65 Which even but now, demanding after you,
Denied me to come in—return, and force
Their scanted courtesy.

KING LEAR: My wits begin to turn.
Come on, my boy: how dost, my boy? art cold?
70 I am cold myself. Where is this straw, my fellow?
The art of our necessities is strange,
That can make vile things precious. Come, your hovel.
Poor fool and knave, I have one part in my heart
That's sorry yet for thee.

I've grown up, I cannot remember ever having experienced such
sheets of fire, such bursts of horrible thunder, and such groans of
roaring wind and rain. The nature of man cannot endure this kind
of anguish or fear!

KING LEAR: Let the great gods, who create this dreadful turmoil over
our heads, discover their enemies now! Tremble, you wretch,
who has committed undisclosed crimes that have not been punished! Hide yourself, you murderer, you liar, you incestuous
impostor of virtue! Fall apart, villain, who has plotted against
man's life with deception and hypocrisy! Secretly hidden guilt,
burst from your hiding-places and beg for mercy from these
dreadful judges! I am a man who's sinned against more than he
has ever sinned.

The more the king loses control the more
he attempts to gain over things
this madness greatens.

KENT: Alas, bare headed! My gracious lord, there is a shed nearby. It will
give you some protection from the storm. Rest there while I return
to this cruel house, whose inhabitants are more hardhearted than
the stones it was built with. Just a short while ago, when I inquired
about you, I was denied access, but I'll demand the courtesy they have
refused to show.

KING LEAR: My mind is beginning to fade. [To the Fool] Come on, my
boy, how are you, my boy? Are you cold? I'm cold myself. [To Kent]
Where is the straw, my friend? The power of hardship is strange. It
can make worthless things seem precious. Come, to this shed. [To
the Fool] Poor fool and knave, there's still a part of my heart that's
sorry for you.

he switches from
enraged to sorry to
enraged to sorry.

75 FOOL: *[Singing]*

> He that has and a little tiny wit—
> With hey, ho, the wind and the rain,—
> Must make content with his fortunes fit,
> For the rain it raineth every day.

80 KING LEAR: True, my good boy. Come, bring us to this hovel.

[Exeunt King Lear and Kent]

FOOL: This is a brave night to cool a courtezan. I'll speak a prophecy
ere I go:

> When priests are more in word than matter;
> When brewers mar their malt with water;
85
> When nobles are their tailors' tutors;
> No heretics burn'd, but wenches' suitors;
> When every case in law is right;
> No squire in debt, nor no poor knight;
> When slanders do not live in tongues;
90
> Nor cutpurses come not to throngs;
> When usurers tell their gold i' the field;
> And bawds and whores do churches build;
> Then shall the realm of Albion
> Come to great confusion:
95
> Then comes the time, who lives to see't,
> That going shall be used with feet.

This prophecy Merlin shall make; for I live before his time.

[Exit]

Fool: [Sings]

> He who has just a little common sense, with
> ho, the wind, and the rain, must make his happi
> adjust to his fortunes, for the rain falls every day

King Lear: True, my good boy. [To Kent] Come, bring us to this shed.

[Lear and Kent exit]

Fool: This is a good night for cooling the lust of a loose woman. I'll make a prophecy before I go:

> When priests say more than they do, when brewers
> mix their malt with water, when nobles teach their
> tailors, when heretics are not burned, but the suitors
> of loose women go up in flames; when every case in
> front of the law is just; when no squire is in debt,
> nor any knight poor; when tongues aren't used to tell
> slanderous stories; when pickpockets don't appear in
> crowds; when gold-diggers openly count their money;
> and bawds and whores endow churches, then the
> British nation will experience confusion; then, the
> time will come, if you're still alive, when walking will
> be done on foot.
> Merlin will one day make this prophecy, because I
> live before his time.

[He exits]

SCENE III

Gloucester's castle.

[Enter Gloucester and Edmund]

GLOUCESTER: Alack, alack, Edmund, I like not this unnatural dealing.
When I desire their leave that I might pity him, they took from
me the use of mine own house; charged me, on pain of their
perpetual displeasure, neither to speak of him, entreat for
5   him, nor any way sustain him.

EDMUND: Most savage and unnatural!

GLOUCESTER: Go to; say you nothing. There's a division betwixt the
dukes; and a worse matter than that: I have received a letter this
night; 'tis dangerous to be spoken; I have locked the letter in my
10   closet: these injuries the king now bears will be revenged home;
there's part of a power already footed: we must incline to the
king. I will seek him, and privily relieve him: go you and maintain talk with the duke, that my charity be not of him perceived:
if he ask for me. I am ill, and gone to bed. Though I die for it,
15   as no less is threatened me, the king my old master must be
relieved. There is some strange thing toward, Edmund; pray
you, be careful.   *[Exit]*

EDMUND: This courtesy, forbid thee, shall the duke
Instantly know; and of that letter too:
20   This seems a fair deserving, and must draw me
That which my father loses; no less than all:
The younger rises when the old doth fall.   *[Exit]*

142

SCENE III

Gloucester's castle.

[Gloucester and Edmund enter]

GLOUCESTER: Alas, alas, Edmund. I don't like this unnatural conduct. When I asked their permission to assist them, they took the use of my own house from me. They commanded me, threatening me with everlasting anger, not to speak of him, plead for him, or provide him with anything necessary.

Gloucester is beginning to experience a taste of what was occurring

EDMUND: Very cruel and unnatural!

GLOUCESTER: Listen, don't say anything. There's a conflict between the dukes, and something even worse. I received a letter tonight. It's dangerous to talk about it. I have locked the letter in my private room. The injustice the king is now suffering will be fully revenged. There's a military force that has already landed. We must side with the king. I will seek him and assist him secretly. You go and maintain all conversation with the duke, so that my help will not be discovered by him. If he asks for me, I'm ill and have gone to bed. Even if I die for it, as I have been threatened, my old master, the king, must receive help. There's something strange about to happen, Edmund. I beg you, be careful.   [He exits]

the king is losing it and needs help.

EDMUND: I'll immediately inform the duke of this kindness, which you have been forbidden to show, and of the letter, too. This seems like an action deserving a reward; it will earn me whatever my father will lose. No less than everything! The young one rises when the old one falls.

[He exits]

Edmund is seeking revenge + greed.

SCENE IV

The heath. Before a hovel.

[Enter King Lear, Kent, and Fool]

KENT: Here is the place, my lord; good my lord, enter:
    The tyranny of the open night's too rough
    For nature to endure.   *[Storm still]*

KING LEAR: Let me alone.

5   KENT: Good my lord, enter here.

KING LEAR: Wilt break my heart?

KENT: I had rather break mine own. Good my lord, enter.

KING LEAR: Thou think'st 'tis much that this contentious storm
    Invades us to the skin: so 'tis to thee;
10   But where the greater malady is fix'd,
    The lesser is scarce felt. Thou'ldst shun a bear;
    But if thy flight lay toward the raging sea,
    Thou'ldst meet the bear i' the mouth. When the mind's free,
    The body's delicate: the tempest in my mind
15   Doth from my senses take all feeling else
    Save what beats there. Filial ingratitude!
    Is it not as this mouth should tear this hand
    For lifting food to't? But I will punish home:
    No, I will weep no more. In such a night
20   To shut me out! Pour on; I will endure.
    In such a night as this! O Regan, Goneril!
    Your old kind father, whose frank heart gave all,—
    O, that way madness lies; let me shun that;
    No more of that.

SCENE IV

The heath. In front of a shed.

[Lear, Kent, and Fool enter]

KENT: *This is the place, my lord. Good, my lord, enter. The torture of a night out in the open is too rough for anyone to endure.*
[The storm continues]

KING LEAR: *Leave me alone.*

KENT: *Good, my lord, enter here.*

KING LEAR: *Will you break my heart?* ——— he is constantly

crying for someone
to truly trust.

KENT: *I'd rather break my own. My good lord, enter.*

KING LEAR: *You think it's unbearable how this hostile storm soaks us to the skin. It is for you, but whenever a greater affliction exists, the lesser can barely be felt. You would avoid a bear, but if your escape lay toward the raging sea, you would confront the bear face-to-face. When the mind is at ease, the body is sensitive. The tempest in my mind overpowers all feelings except for the pain in my heart. The ingratitude of children! Isn't it as if this mouth would bite off this hand for lifting food to it? But I will punish thoroughly! No, I won't cry anymore. To lock me out on such a night! Pour on, rain! I will endure it. On a night like this one! Oh, Regan, Goneril! Your old, kind father, whose generous heart gave you everything—oh, thinking about this will lead to madness. Let me avoid it; no more of that.*

Sense of self

he admits thinking of how he trusted them will lead him to more madness.

145

KENT: Good my lord, enter here.

KING LEAR: Prithee, go in thyself: seek thine own ease:
This tempest will not give me leave to ponder
On things would hurt me more. But I'll go in.
[To the Fool] In, boy; go first. You houseless poverty,—
30 Nay, get thee in. I'll pray, and then I'll sleep.   *[Fool goes in]*
Poor naked wretches, whereso'er you are,
That bide the pelting of this pitiless storm,
How shall your houseless heads and unfed sides,
Your loop'd and window'd raggedness, defend you
35 From seasons such as these? O, I have ta'en
Too little care of this! Take physic, pomp;
Expose thyself to feel what wretches feel,
That thou mayst shake the superflux to them,
And show the heavens more just.

40 EDGAR: *[Within]* Fathom and half, fathom and half! Poor Tom!
                    [The Fool runs out from the hovel]

FOOL: Come not in here, nuncle, here's a spirit
Help me, help me!

KENT: Give me thy hand. Who's there?

FOOL: A spirit, a spirit: he says his name's poor Tom.

45 KENT: What art thou that dost grumble there i' the straw?
Come forth.

[Enter Edgar disguised as a mad man]

EDGAR: Away! the foul fiend follows me!
Through the sharp hawthorn blows the cold wind.
Hum! go to thy cold bed, and warm thee.

KENT: *Good, my lord, enter here.*

KING LEAR: *Please, go in yourself! Seek your own comfort. This tempest will keep me from thinking about things that would hurt me even more. But I'll go inside.* [To the Fool] *In, boy, go first. You poor creature! Come, get yourself inside. I'll pray, and then I'll sleep.* [Fool goes inside]
Poor, naked wretches, wherever you are, who endure the pounding of this merciless storm. How will your uncovered heads and starving bodies, your torn and tattered clothes protect you from weather like this? Oh, I have cared too little about this! Experience this, oh you wealthy people Expose yourselves to feel what poor people feel, so that you may give your superfluous wealth to them and prove that the gods are just.

[handwritten margin note: he cares for most who show the weighest bit of care.]

EDGAR: [Heard from inside. Muttering madly] *Fathom and a half, fathom and a half. Poor Tom.*
[The Fool comes running out of the shed]

FOOL: *Don't come in, my uncle, there's a ghost. Help me, help me!*

KENT: *Give me your hand. Who's there?*

FOOL: *A ghost, a ghost. He says his name is poor Tom.*

KENT: *Who is this muttering there in the straw? Come out!*

[Edgar enters, disguised as a madman]

EDGAR: *Keep away! The foul fiend follows me! The cold wind blows through the sharp hawthorn bush! Hmm. Go to your warm bed and warm yourself.*

50   KING LEAR: Hast thou given all to thy two daughters?
      And art thou come to this?

  EDGAR: Who gives any thing to poor Tom? whom the foul fiend hath
      led through fire and through flame, and through ford and whir-
      lipool e'er bog and quagmire; that hath laid knives under his pil-
      low, and halters in his pew; set ratsbane by his porridge; made
55   film proud of heart, to ride on a bay trotting-horse over
      four-inched bridges, to course his own shadow for a traitor.
      Bless thy five wits! Tom's a-cold,—O, do de, do de, do de. Bless
      thee from whirlwinds, star-blasting, and taking! Do poor Tom
      some charity, whom the foul fiend vexes: there could I have him
60   now,—and there,—and there again, and there.   *[Storm still]*

  KING LEAR: What, have his daughters brought him to this pass?
      Couldst thou save nothing? Didst thou give them all?

  FOOL: Nay, he reserved a blanket, else we had been all shamed.

  KING LEAR: Now, all the plagues that in the pendulous air
65   Hang fated o'er men's faults light on thy daughters!

  KENT: He hath no daughters, sir.

  KING LEAR: Death, traitor! nothing could have subdued nature
      To such a lowness but his unkind daughters.
      Is it the fashion, that discarded fathers
70   Should have thus little mercy on their flesh?
      Judicious punishment! 'twas this flesh begot
      Those pelican daughters.

Have you given everything to

Act I

KING LEAR: Have you given everything to your two daug
you ended up here?

EDGAR: Who gives anything to poor Tom, whom the ,
through fire and through flames, through fords and wh...
through marshes and swamps? He has placed knives under his pil-
low and hung ropes from the church balcony. He has put poison in
his soup, became proud enough to ride a brown trotting-horse over
narrow bridges, to chase his own shadow as if he was a traitor. Bless
your five wits! Tom's cold! Oh, do de, o, do de, do de. Protect yourself
from whirlwinds, evil stars, and bewitchment. Help poor Tom, who is
plagued by the foul fiend! [He slaps at an imaginary attacker] There,
I'll get you now! And there, again! And there!

[The storm still rages]

KING LEAR: What, have his daughters brought him into this predicament?
Could you save anything? Did you give them everything?

FOOL: No, he kept a blanket for himself, or we all would have felt ashamed.

KING LEAR: May all the diseases that linger fatefully in the swaying air
over men's faults now come down on your daughters.

KENT: He has no daughters, sir.

KING LEAR: Death to you, traitor! Nothing could have reduced this man
to this degenerate state but his unkind daughters. Is it the fashion
nowadays that rejected fathers should have so little mercy on their
flesh? Rightful punishment! It was this flesh that fathered these
blood-thirsty daughters.

he has immediate anger towards any possible
betrayal he may face... madness
ensues.

149

EDGAR: Pillicock sat on Pillicock-hill:
            Halloo, halloo, loo, loo!

75 FOOL: This cold night will turn us all to fools and madmen.

EDGAR: Take heed o' the foul fiend: obey thy parents; keep thy word
    justly; swear not; commit not with man's sworn spouse; set not
    thy sweet heart on proud array. Tom's a-cold.

KING LEAR: What hast thou been?

80 EDGAR: A serving-man, proud in heart and mind; that curled my
    hair; wore gloves in my cap; served the lust of my mistress'
    heart, and did the act of darkness with her; swore as many oaths
    as I spake words, and broke them in the sweet face of heaven:
    one that slept in the contriving of lust, and waked to do it: wine
85 loved I deeply, dice dearly: and in woman out-paramoured the
    Turk: false of heart, light of ear, bloody of hand; hog in sloth,
    fox in stealth, wolf in greediness, dog in madness, lion in prey.
    Let not the creaking of shoes nor the rustling of silks betray thy
    poor heart to woman: keep thy foot out of brothels, thy hand
90 out of plackets, thy pen from lenders' books, and defy the foul
    fiend.
            Still through the hawthorn blows the cold wind:
            Says suum, mun, ha, no, nonny.
    Dauphin, my boy, my boy, sessa! let him trot by.
                                                    [Storm still]

95 KING LEAR: Why, thou wert better in thy grave than to answer with
    thy uncovered body this extremity of the skies. Is man no more
    than this? Consider him well. Thou owest the worm no silk, the
    beast no hide, the sheep no wool, the cat no perfume. Ha! here's
    three on 's are sophisticated! Thou art the thing itself:

EDGAR: [Reciting a nursery rhyme] *Pillicock sat*
Halloo, halloo, loo, loo!

FOOL: *This cold night will turn all of us into fools and madmen.*

EDGAR: *Beware of the foul fiend! Obey your parents, tell only the truth,*
don't swear, don't commit adultery, and don't long for luxurious
clothes. Tom's cold.

KING LEAR: *What did you used to be?*

EDGAR: *A servant, proud in my heart and mind. I curled my hair,*
received love-tokens from my mistress, satisfied my mistress' pas-
sion, and lay with her at night. I swore an oath whenever I spoke
and broke all of them while the gods were looking on. When I
slept, I dreamed up lustful scenarios, and I lived them out when I
woke up. I loved wine and gambling and had more mistresses than
the Sultan. I had a lying disposition, was interested in gossip, and
attracted to violence. I was as lazy as a pig, deceitful as a fox,
greedy as a wolf, mad as a dog, and barbaric as a lion. Don't let the
creaking of shoes or the rustling of silk fool you into giving your
heart to women. Keep out of brothels, keep your hand away from
petticoats, and your signature away from the books of moneylend-
ers, and defy the foul fiend.
> *The cold wind still blows through the hawthorn*
> *bushes. It says, "Suum, mun, ha, no, nonny." My*
> *horse, my boy, my boy!*
Let him trot by.   [The storm still rages]

KING LEAR: *You'd be better off in your grave than to face this extreme*
violence with your unprotected body! Is man not better than
this? Pay close attention. You don't owe the silkworm anything
for its silk, or the beast for its fur, or the sheep for its wool, or
the civet cat for its perfume. Ha! Here are three of us who are
corrupted. You are the essential being: A simple, unfurnished

151

unaccommodated man is no more but such a poor bare, forked
animal as thou art. Off, off, you lendings! come unbutton here.

[Tearing off his clothes]

Fool: Prithee, nuncle, be contented; 'tis a naughty night to swim in.
Now a little fire in a wild field were like an old lecher's heart;
a small spark, all the rest on's body cold. Look, here comes a
105   walking fire.

[Enter Gloucester, with a torch]

Edgar: This is the foul fiend Flibbertigibbet: he begins at curfew,
and walks till the first cock; he gives the web and the pin,
squints the eye, and makes the hare-lip; mildews the white
wheat, and hurts the poor creature of earth.
110   Saint Withold footed thrice the old;
        He met the night-mare, and her nine-fold;
            Bid her alight,
            And her troth plight,
        And, aroint thee, witch, aroint thee!

115 Kent: How fares your grace?

King Lear: What's he?

Kent: Who's there? What is't you seek?

Gloucester: What are you there? Your names?

Edgar: Poor Tom; that eats the swimming frog, the toad, the tad-
120   pole, the wall-newt and the water; that in the fury of his heart,
when the foul fiend rages, eats cow-dung for sallets; swallows
the old rat and the ditch-dog; drinks the green mantle of the
standing pool; who is whipped from tithing to tithing, and
stock-punished, and imprisoned; who hath had three suits to
125   his back, six shirts to his body, horse to ride, and weapon to
wear;

152

*man is no more than a poor, bare, two-legged animal such
as you are. Off, off, you borrowed garments! Come unbutton
here!*   [Lear is tearing off his clothes]

FOOL: *Please, uncle, stop this. It's a nasty night for taking a swim. A
little fire in the uncultivated countryside is like the heart of a lecher.
A small spark of feeling, while all the rest of his body is cold. Look,
here comes a walking fire!*

[Gloucester enters with a torch]

EDGAR: *This is the foul fiend, the demon Flibbertigibbet! He comes out at
nightfall and walks about till midnight. He gives cataracts, causes
strains to the eye and harelips. He mildews the ripening wheat and
tortures the poor creatures of the earth.*
> *Saint Withold walked across the plain three times. He
> met the night-mare and her nine offspring. Bid her to
> let go and do no harm. Be gone witch, be gone!*

KENT: *How is your Grace doing?*

KING LEAR: *Who's he?*

KENT: [To Gloucester] *Who's there? What is it you want?*

GLOUCESTER: *Who are you there? Your names?*

EDGAR: *Poor Tom, who eats the swimming frog, the toad, the tadpole,
the lizard, and the water-newt. Out of anger, when the foul fiend
rages, he eats cow-dung instead of salad. He swallows the old rat
and the dog lying in the ditch. He drinks the green scum from
standing waters. He is chased from one district to the next, put in
stocks, and imprisoned. He used to own three suits and six shirts,
a horse, and a weapon.*

But mice and rats, and such small deer,
Have been Tom's food for seven long year.
Beware my follower. Peace, Smulkin; peace, thou fiend!

130   GLOUCESTER: What, hath your grace no better company?

EDGAR: The prince of darkness is a gentleman:
Modo he's call'd, and Mahu.

GLOUCESTER: Our flesh and blood is grown so vile, my lord,
That it doth hate what gets it.

135   EDGAR: Poor Tom's a-cold.

GLOUCESTER: Go in with me: my duty cannot suffer
To obey in all your daughters' hard commands:
Though their injunction be to bar my doors,
And let this tyrannous night take hold upon you,
140   Yet have I ventured to come seek you out,
And bring you where both fire and food is ready.

KING LEAR: First let me talk with this philosopher.
What is the cause of thunder?

KENT: Good my lord, take his offer; go into the house.

145   KING LEAR: I'll talk a word with this same learned Theban.
What is your study?

EDGAR: How to prevent the fiend, and to kill vermin.

KING LEAR: Let me ask you one word in private.

KENT: Importune him once more to go, my lord;
150   His wits begin to unsettle.

154

But mice and rats, and small animals have been Tom's
food for the past seven years.
Beware, my followers! [He talks as if to an imaginary fiend] Be
quiet, Smulkin, be quiet, you fiend.

GLOUCESTER: *What, does your Grace not have better company?*

EDGAR: *The devil is a gentleman; he's called Modo and Mahu.*

GLOUCESTER: *Our children have turned out so evil that they hate their*
parents.

EDGAR: *Poor Tom's cold.*

GLOUCESTER: *Come in with me. My duty does not allow me to endure all*
your daughters' harsh commands. Although they ordered me to lock
my door and let this horrible night take advantage of you, yet I've
ventured to find you and bring you to a place where a fire and food
are awaiting you.

KING LEAR: *First, let me talk to this scientist. What is the cause of*
thunder?

KENT: *My good lord, take his offer. Go into the house.*

KING LEAR: *I'll have a word with this learned scholar. What is your spe-*
cial field of knowledge?

EDGAR: *How to thwart the devil and kill vermin.*

KING LEAR: *Let me ask you something in private.*

KENT: *Urge him one more time to go, my lord. His mind begins to*
fade.

GLOUCESTER: Canst thou blame him?

[Storm still]

His daughters seek his death: ah, that good Kent!
He said it would be thus, poor banish'd man!
Thou say'st the king grows mad; I'll tell thee, friend,
155   I am almost mad myself: I had a son,
Now outlaw'd from my blood; he sought my life,
But lately, very late: I loved him, friend;
No father his son dearer: truth to tell thee,
The grief hath crazed my wits. What a night's this!
160   I do beseech your grace,—

KING LEAR: O, cry your mercy, sir.
Noble philosopher, your company.

EDGAR: Tom's a-cold.

GLOUCESTER: In, fellow, there, into the hovel: keep thee warm.

165   KING LEAR: Come let's in all.

KENT: This way, my lord.

KING LEAR: With him;
I will keep still with my philosopher.

KENT: Good my lord, soothe him; let him take the fellow.

170   GLOUCESTER: Take him you on.

KENT: Sirrah, come on; go along with us.

KING LEAR: Come, good Athenian.

GLOUCESTER: *Can you blame him?* [The storm continues] *His daughters want him dead. Ah, good Kent. He predicted that it would come to this. Poor banished man! You say the king is going mad. I'll tell you, my friend, I'm almost mad myself. I had a son, who has been banished and disinherited. He tried to kill me, only very recently. I loved him, my friend; no father ever loved his son more. To tell you the truth, the grief has been driving me crazy. What a night this is! I beg your Grace—*

KING LEAR: *Oh, I beg your pardon, sir.* [To Edgar] *Noble scientist, please give us your company!*

EDGAR: *Tom's cold!*

GLOUCESTER: *Go inside, fellow, there, into the shed. Keep yourself warm.*

KING LEAR: *Come, let's all go in.*

KENT: *This way, my lord.*

KING LEAR: *With him; I will keep close to my philosopher.*

KENT: [To Gloucester] *Good, my lord, humor him. Let him take the fellow.*

GLOUCESTER: *You take care of him.*

KENT: *Sir, come on, come along with us.*

KING LEAR: *Come, good philosopher.*

GLOUCESTER: No words, no words: hush.

EDGAR: Child Rowland to the dark tower came,
175   His word was still,—Fie, foh, and fum,
     I smell the blood of a British man.

[Exeunt]

SCENE V

Gloucester's castle.

[Enter Cornwall and Edmund]

CORNWALL: I will have my revenge ere I depart his house.

EDMUND: How, my lord, I may be censured, that nature thus gives
    way to loyalty, something fears me to think of.

5 CORNWALL: I now perceive, it was not altogether your brother's evil
    disposition made him seek his death; but a provoking merit, set
    a-work by a reprovable badness in himself.

EDMUND: How malicious is my fortune, that I must repent to be just!
    This is the letter he spoke of, which approves him an intelligent
10   party to the advantages of France: O heavens! that this treason
    were not, or not I the detector!

CORNWALL: Go with me to the duchess.

EDMUND: If the matter of this paper be certain, you have mighty
    business in hand.

GLOUCESTER: *No speaking, no speaking, hush.*

EDGAR: *Child Rowland came to the dark tower. His words were "fie, foh, and fum, I smell the blood of a British man!"*

[All exit]

- king lear's madness makes him numb to the storm: a loss of sense of self

storm ⟷ lear's mental state.

SCENE V

Gloucester's castle.

[Cornwall and Edmund enter]

CORNWALL: *I'll have my revenge before I leave this house.*

EDMUND: *My lord, it frightens me to think how I will be judged for putting loyalty above the affection for my father.*

CORNWALL: *I now understand that it was not only your brother Edgar's evil disposition that made him seek your father's death. He was provoked because his father deserved it and then inspired by his own evil inclination.*

EDMUND: *How tragically unfortunate I am, because I have to regret doing the right thing. This is the letter he told me about, which proves that he was passing information to aid the king of France. Oh heavens. I wish this wasn't treason. I wish I hadn't discovered it.*

CORNWALL: *Follow me to the Duchess.*

EDMUND: *If the meaning of this letter can be confirmed, you have a lot of work to do.*

15 CORNWALL: True or false, it hath made thee earl of Gloucester. Seek
    out where thy father is, that he may be ready for our apprehen-
    sion.

    EDMUND: *[Aside]* If I find him comforting the king, it will stuff his
    suspicion more fully.—I will persevere in my course of loyalty,
20 though the conflict be sore between that and my blood.

    CORNWALL: I will lay trust upon thee; and thou shalt find a dearer
    father in my love.   *[Exeunt]*

SCENE VI

A chamber in a farmhouse adjoining the castle.

[Enter Gloucester, King Lear, Kent, Fool, and Edgar]

GLOUCESTER: Here is better than the open air; take it thankfully. I
    will piece out the comfort with what addition I can: I will not
    be long from you.

    KENT: All the power of his wits have given way to his impatience:
5   the gods reward your kindness!
                                        [Exit Gloucester]

    EDGAR: Frateretto calls me; and tells me
    Nero is an angler in the lake of darkness.
    Pray, innocent, and beware the foul fiend.

    FOOL: Prithee, nuncle, tell me whether a madman be a gentleman or
10 a yeoman?

160

CORNWALL: *Whether it's true or not, it has made you the Earl of Gloucester. Find out where your father is, so he will be available for his arrest.*

EDMUND: [Aside] *If I find him helping the king, it will add to the duke's suspicion of him. I will continue in my loyal course, though it will cause a painful conflict between my duty and my family.*

CORNWALL: *I will put trust in you, and you will find I'll be a better father to you.*

[They exit]

SCENE VI

A chamber in the farmhouse adjoining the castle.

[Gloucester, Lear, Kent (disguised), Fool, and Edgar enter]

GLOUCESTER: *It's better here than outside. Be grateful for it. I will make it more comfortable with whatever else I can find. I won't be gone for long.*

KENT: *His mind is fading in the face of this hardship. May the gods reward your kindness!*

[Gloucester exits]

EDGAR: *The devil Frateretto calls me and tells me Nero is fishing in the lake of darkness. [To the FOOL] Be careful, innocent one, and beware of the foul fiend!*

FOOL: *Tell me, uncle, whether a madman is a gentleman or a yeoman.*

KING LEAR: A king, a king!

FOOL: No, he's a yeoman that has a gentleman to his son; for he's a
    mad yeoman that sees his son a gentleman before him.

KING LEAR: To have a thousand with red burning spits
15   Come hissing in upon 'em,—

EDGAR: The foul fiend bites my back.

FOOL: He's mad that trusts in the tameness of a wolf, a horse's
    health, a boy's love, or a whore's oath.

KING LEAR: It shall be done; I will arraign them straight.
20   [To Edgar] Come, sit thou here, most learned justicer;
    [To the Fool] Thou, sapient sir, sit here. Now, you she foxes!

EDGAR: Look, where he stands and glares!
    Wantest thou eyes at trial, madam?
    [Singing] Come o'er the bourn, Bessy, to me,—

FOOL:
25   Her boat hath a leak,
            And she must not speak
            Why she dares not come over to thee.

EDGAR: The foul fiend haunts poor Tom in the voice of a night-
    ingale. Hopdance cries in Tom's belly for two white herring.
30   Croak not, black angel; I have no food for thee.

KENT: How do you, sir? Stand you not so amazed:
    Will you lie down and rest upon the cushions?

KING LEAR: A king, a king!

FOOL: No, he's a yeoman if his son becomes a gentleman. ｜ yeoman, if he makes his son into a gentleman before he becomes one himself.

KING LEAR: [Thinking about his daughters] *To have a thousand devils with burning red sticks running after them.*

sought revenge/ madness/ rationality

EDGAR: The foul fiend is biting my back!

FOOL: Anyone is mad who trusts in the tameness of a wolf, a horse's health, the love of a boy, or an oath sworn by a whore!

anyone is mad who trusts in the one bound to play you.

KING LEAR: It shall be done! I'll indict them immediately! [To Edgar] Come, you sit here, most learned judge. [To the Fool] You, wise sir, sit here. Now, you she-foxes.

EDGAR: Look where he stands and glares. [Addressing the imaginary accused] Do you want spectators at your trial, madam?
Come over the stream, Bessy, to me.

FOOL: [Sings]
Her boat has a leak, and she is not allowed to tell why
she doesn't dare to come over to you.

EDGAR: The foul fiend haunts poor Tom, singing like a nightingale. The dancing fiend Hopdance cries inside of Tom's belly for two fresh herrings. Stop complaining, black angel, I have no food for you.

KENT: How are you doing, sir? Don't stand there in bewilderment. Will you lie down and rest on these cushions?

KING LEAR: I'll see their trial first. Bring in the evidence.
    [To Edgar] Thou robed man of justice, take thy place;
35   *[To the Fool]* And thou, his yoke-fellow of equity,
    Bench by his side: *[To Kent]* you are o' the commission,
    Sit you too.

EDGAR: Let us deal justly.
        Sleepest or wakest thou, jolly shepherd?
40   Thy sheep be in the corn;
        And for one blast of thy minikin mouth,
          Thy sheep shall take no harm.
    Pur! the cat is gray.

KING LEAR: Arraign her first; 'tis Goneril. I here take my oath before
45   this honourable assembly, she kicked the poor king her father.

FOOL: Come hither, mistress. Is your name Goneril?

KING LEAR: She cannot deny it.

FOOL: Cry you mercy, I took you for a joint-stool.

KING LEAR: And here's another, whose warp'd looks proclaim
50   What store her heart is made on. Stop her there!
    Arms, arms, sword, fire! Corruption in the place!
    False justicer, why hast thou let her 'scape?

EDGAR: Bless thy five wits!

KENT: O pity! Sir, where is the patience now,
55   That thou so oft have boasted to retain?

EDGAR: *[Aside]* My tears begin to take his part so much,
    They'll mar my counterfeiting.

KING LEAR: I'll oversee their trial first. Bring in the witnesses against them. [To Edgar] *Take your seat, judge dressed in your robes.* [To the Fool] *And you, his partner, take your seat on the bench next to him.* [To Kent] *You belong to the commission of justices of the peace. Sit as well.*

EDGAR: *Let us handle the case justly.* [He sings]
> Are you sleeping, or are you awake, jolly shepherd?
> Your sheep are in the cornfield, and if you call them
> back with your pretty mouth, we will not harm them.
Purr, the devilish cat, is gray.

KING LEAR: *Prosecute her first! It's Goneril. I hereby swear under oath in front of this honorable assembly that she kicked the poor king, her father.*

FOOL: *Come here, mistress! Is your name Goneril?*

KING LEAR: *She cannot deny it!*

FOOL: *I beg your pardon! I mistook you for a stool!*

KING LEAR: *And here is another one whose nasty glances reveal what her heart is made of. Stop her! Weapons, weapons, sword, fire! There's corruption in the court! False judge, why did you let her escape?*

his named for the ones he once trusted.

EDGAR: *Bless your senses.*

KENT: *Have mercy. Sir, where is your patience now that you have so often bragged about?*

EDGAR: [Aside] *My tears openly show my sympathy for him. They'll ruin my disguise.*

KING LEAR: The little dogs and all, Tray, Blanch, and
    Sweet-heart, see, they bark at me.

60 EDGAR: Tom will throw his head at them. Avaunt, you curs!
        Be thy mouth or black or white,
        Tooth that poisons if it bite;
        Mastiff, grey-hound, mongrel grim,
        Hound or spaniel, brach or lym,
65   Or bobtail tike or trundle-tail,
        Tom will make them weep and wail:
        For, with throwing thus my head,
        Dogs leap the hatch, and all are fled.
    Do de, de, de. Sessa! Come, march to wakes and fairs and mar-
    ket-towns. Poor Tom, thy horn is dry.

70 KING LEAR: Then let them anatomize Regan; see what breeds about
    her heart. Is there any cause in nature that makes these hard
    hearts? *[To Edgar]* You, sir, I entertain for one of my hundred;
    only I do not like the fashion of your garments: you will say
    they are Persian attire: but let them be changed.

75 KENT: Now, good my lord, lie here and rest awhile.

KING LEAR: Make no noise, make no noise; draw the curtains: so, so,
    so. We'll go to supper i' he morning. So, so, so.

FOOL: And I'll go to bed at noon.

[Re-enter Gloucester]

GLOUCESTER: Come hither, friend: where is the king my master?

80 KENT: Here, sir; but trouble him not, his wits are gone.

GLOUCESTER: Good friend, I prithee, take him in thy arms;
    I have o'erheard a plot of death upon him:
    There is a litter ready; lay him in 't,

KING LEAR: *The little dogs, Trey, Blanch, and Sweetheart, are barking at me!*

EDGAR: *Tom will fight them off. Stay away, you dogs!*
> *Whether your mouth is black or white, with teeth that poison when they bite, mastiff, greyhound, grim mongrel, hound or spaniel, bitch hound, or bloodhound, short-tailed pup, or long-tailed dog, Tom will make them weep and cry. If I throw my head like this, dogs run outside, and all are fled.*
Do de, de, de. Come, visit parish festivals, fairs, and market-towns! Poor Tom, your cup is empty.

KING LEAR: *Then let them dissect Regan. See what's brooding in her heart. Is there any natural cause for these hard hearts? [To Edgar] You, sir, I'll take you into my service as one of my hundred followers, but I don't like your clothes. You'll say that they're Persian, but please change them.*

KENT: *Now, my good lord, lie here and rest for a while.*

KING LEAR: *Make no noise, make no noise. Draw the curtains, so, so, so. We'll eat supper in the morning. So, so, so.*

FOOL: *And I'll go to bed at noon.*

[Gloucester enters]

GLOUCESTER: *Come here, my friend, where is the king, my master?*

KENT: *Here, sir, but don't disturb him. His mind is gone!*

GLOUCESTER: *Good friend, I beg you, take him in your arms. I have heard about a plot to murder him. A stretcher is ready. Lay him*

167

85 And drive towards Dover, friend, where thou shalt meet
Both welcome and protection. Take up thy master:
If thou shouldst dally half an hour, his life,
With thine, and all that offer to defend him,
Stand in assured loss: take up, take up;
And follow me, that will to some provision
90 Give thee quick conduct.

KENT: Oppressed nature sleeps:
This rest might yet have balm'd thy broken senses,
Which, if convenience will not allow,
Stand in hard cure.
95 *[To the Fool]* Come, help to bear thy master;
Thou must not stay behind.

GLOUCESTER: Come, come, away.
                         [Exeunt all but Edgar]

EDGAR: When we our betters see bearing our woes,
We scarcely think our miseries our foes.
100 Who alone suffers suffers most i' the mind,
Leaving free things and happy shows behind:
But then the mind much sufferance doth o'er skip,
When grief hath mates, and bearing fellowship.
How light and portable my pain seems now,
105 When that which makes me bend makes the king bow,
He childed as I father'd! Tom, away!
Mark the high noises; and thyself bewray,
When false opinion, whose wrong thought defiles thee,
In thy just proof, repeals and reconciles thee.
110 What will hap more to-night, safe 'scape the king!
Lurk, lurk.
                               [Exit]

on it and drive to Dover, my friend, where you will be welcome and find protection. Take your master. If you wait for only half an hour, his life, and yours, and the lives of all who offer to defend him, will certainly be lost. Take him, take him, and follow me. I'll lead you quickly to some necessary supplies for the journey.

KENT: *His torture has put him to sleep. This rest might yet heal his shattered nerves. If the situation doesn't allow for that, they might be hard to cure.* [To the Fool] *Come; help me carry your master. You can't stay behind.*

GLOUCESTER: *Come, come, let's go!*

[Exit all but Edgar]

EDGAR: *When we see our superiors suffering troubles like ours, we almost forget about our own misery. He, who suffers alone, has the greatest mental suffering and forgets about carefree times and happiness. But the mind neglects some of the suffering, whenever grief and suffering have company. How easy and bearable my pain now seems, when the king breaks under the burden that strikes me. He has been banished by his children, as I have been banished by my father. Tom, leave. Pay attention to the rumors and reveal yourself as soon as the false claims that have injured you have been proven to be untrue, and you are restored to favor. Whatever else happens tonight, may the king escapes safely. Keep out of sight! Keep out of sight!*

[He exits]

3.6 shows lear's madness in his hallucination + desire to have fake trials for his daughters.

SCENE VII

Gloucester's castle.

[Enter Cornwall, Regan, Goneril, Edmund, and Servants]

CORNWALL: Post speedily to my lord your husband; show him
    this letter: the army of France is landed. Seek out the villain
    Gloucester.

                           [Exeunt some of the Servants]

REGAN: Hang him instantly.

5   GONERIL: Pluck out his eyes.

CORNWALL: Leave him to my displeasure. Edmund, keep you our
    sister company: the revenges we are bound to take upon your
    traitorous father are not fit for your beholding. Advise the duke,
    where you are going, to a most festinate preparation: we are
10   bound to the like. Our posts shall be swift and intelligent betwixt
    us. Farewell, dear sister: farewell, my lord of Gloucester.

[Enter Oswald]
    How now! where's the king?

OSWALD: My lord of Gloucester hath convey'd him hence:
    Some five or six and thirty of his knights,
15   Hot questrists after him, met him at gate;
    Who, with some other of the lords dependants,
    Are gone with him towards Dover; where they boast
    To have well-armed friends.

CORNWALL: Get horses for your mistress.

SCENE VII

Gloucester's castle.

[Cornwall, Regan, Goneril, Edmund, and Servants enter]

CORNWALL: [To Goneril] *Hurry quickly to my lord, your husband. Show him this letter (the letter Edmund took from Gloucester's room). France's army has arrived! Find Gloucester, the traitor!*
[Some Servants exit]

REGAN: *Hang him immediately!*

GONERIL: *Pluck his eyes out!*

CORNWALL: *Leave him to my anger! Edmund, keep our sister-in-law company. The revengeful act we have in mind for your father is not suitable for you to witness. Tell the duke, when you see him, to prepare for war quickly. We will likewise prepare for war. Our messengers will deliver information between the two of us quickly. Farewell, dear sister-in-law. Farewell, my lord of Gloucester.*

[Oswald enters]
Well. Where's the king?

OSWALD: *The Lord of Gloucester has led him away. About thirty-five or thirty-six of his knights, who had been searching for him, met him at the gates. Together with a few more of Lord Gloucester's men, they have gone to Dover with him. They claim to have well-armed friends there.*

CORNWALL: *Get horses ready for your mistress.*

171

20   GONERIL: Farewell, sweet lord, and sister.

CORNWALL: Edmund, farewell.
                    [Exeunt Goneril, Edmund, and Oswald]
                Go seek the traitor Gloucester,
        Pinion him like a thief, bring him before us.
                            [Exeunt other Servants]
        Though well we may not pass upon his life
25   Without the form of justice, yet our power
        Shall do a courtesy to our wrath, which men
        May blame, but not control. Who's there? the traitor?

[Enter Gloucester, brought in by two or three]

REGAN: Ingrateful fox! 'tis he.

CORNWALL: Bind fast his corky arms.

30   GLOUCESTER: What mean your graces? Good my friends, consider
        You are my guests: do me no foul play, friends.

CORNWALL: Bind him, I say.   *[Servants bind him]*

REGAN: Hard, hard. O filthy traitor!

GLOUCESTER: Unmerciful lady as you are, I'm none.

35   CORNWALL: To this chair bind him. Villain, thou shalt find—
                            [Regan plucks his beard]

GLOUCESTER: By the kind gods, 'tis most ignobly done
        To pluck me by the beard.

REGAN: So white, and such a traitor!

172

GONERIL: *Farewell, my sweet lord, and sister.*

CORNWALL: *Edmund, farewell.*
[Goneril, Edmund, and Oswald exit]
Go seek Gloucester, the traitor. Tie him up like a thief, and bring him to us! [All other Servants exit]

Although we may not be able to sentence him to death without a formal trial, we're powerful enough to do our anger justice. We may be blamed for it, but we won't be stopped. Who's there? The traitor?

[Gloucester enters, brought in by two or three men]

REGAN: *The ungrateful fox! It's him.*

CORNWALL: *Tie his withered arms tightly.*

GLOUCESTER: *What do your Graces mean? My good friends, -consider that you are my guests! Don't treat me unfairly, my friends!*

CORNWALL: *Tie him up, I say!* [Servants tie him up]

REGAN: *Tight! Tight! Oh, you filthy traitor!*

GLOUCESTER: *You unmerciful lady! I'm no traitor!*

CORNWALL: *Tie him to this chair. Villain, you will find—*
[Regan plucks his beard]

GLOUCESTER: *By god, it's very degrading to pluck my beard!*

REGAN: *So white, and such a traitor!*

GLOUCESTER: Naughty lady,

40   These hairs, which thou dost ravish from my chin,
    Will quicken, and accuse thee: I am your host:
    With robbers' hands my hospitable favours
    You should not ruffle thus. What will you do?

CORNWALL: Come, sir, what letters had you late from France?

45 REGAN: Be simple answerer, for we know the truth.

CORNWALL: And what confederacy have you with the traitors
    Late footed in the kingdom?

REGAN: To whose hands have you sent the lunatic king? Speak.

GLOUCESTER: I have a letter guessingly set down,
50   Which came from one that's of a neutral heart,
    And not from one opposed.

CORNWALL: Cunning.

REGAN: And false.

CORNWALL: Where hast thou sent the king?

55 GLOUCESTER: To Dover.

REGAN: Wherefore to Dover? Wast thou not charged at peril—

CORNWALL: Wherefore to Dover? Let him first answer that.

GLOUCESTER: I am tied to the stake, and I must stand the course.

REGAN: Wherefore to Dover, sir?

174

GLOUCESTER: Wicked lady! These hairs that you pluck out of my chin will come to life and accuse you. I'm your host. You should not attack the hospitality I have shown you like robbers! What are you going to do?

CORNWALL: Come, sir. What letter have you recently received from the king of France?

REGAN: Give a straight answer because we know the truth.

CORNWALL: And what alliance do you have with the traitors who have recently set foot into our kingdom?

REGAN: Where have you sent the crazy king? Speak!

GLOUCESTER: I have a speculative letter that came from a neutral source, not from an enemy.

CORNWALL: Ingenious.

REGAN: And a lie!

CORNWALL: Where have you sent the king?

GLOUCESTER: To Dover.

REGAN: Why to Dover? Weren't you told under threat of punishment—

CORNWALL: Why to Dover? Let him answer that first.

GLOUCESTER: I am tied to the stake, and I must endure the attack.

REGAN: Why to Dover, sir?

60   GLOUCESTER: Because I would not see thy cruel nails
        Pluck out his poor old eyes; nor thy fierce sister
        In his anointed flesh stick boarish fangs.
        The sea, with such a storm as his bare head
        In hell-black night endured, would have buoy'd up,
65   And quench'd the stelled fires:
        Yet, poor old heart, he holp the heavens to rain.
        If wolves had at thy gate howl'd that stern time,
        Thou shouldst have said 'Good porter, turn the key,'
        All cruels else subscribed: but I shall see
70   The winged vengeance overtake such children.

    CORNWALL: See't shalt thou never. Fellows, hold the chair.
        Upon these eyes of thine I'll set my foot.

    GLOUCESTER: He that will think to live till he be old,
        Give me some help! O cruel! O you gods!

75   REGAN: One side will mock another; the other too.

    CORNWALL: If you see vengeance,—

    FIRST SERVANT: Hold your hand, my lord:
        I have served you ever since I was a child;
        But better service have I never done you
80   Than now to bid you hold.

    REGAN: How now, you dog!

    FIRST SERVANT: If you did wear a beard upon your chin,
        I'd shake it on this quarrel. What do you mean?

    CORNWALL: My villain!   *[They draw and fight]*

85   FIRST SERVANT: Nay, then, come on, and take the chance of anger.

176

GLOUCESTER: Because I could not stand by and watch your cruel nails pluck out his poor old eyes, nor watch your brutal sister strike his anointed body with her boar-like tusks. In such a storm as the one he had to endure without protection on a night as dark as hell—the sea would have risen up and put out the fires of the stars. Yet, the poor old heart, he cried alongside the rain. If wolves had howled at your gate on this dreadful night, you would have said, "Good porter, unlock the door and let them in." All other cruel beings would feel pity, but I'll see the vengeance of the gods come down on children like you.

think of "the storm" as his mind.

CORNWALL: You will never see it! Fellows, hold the chair! I'll push my foot on your eyes!

GLOUCESTER: Anyone who hopes to become old, give me some help! Oh cruel! Oh you gods!

REGAN: One side will mock the other! The other, too!

CORNWALL: If you see vengeance—

FIRST SERVANT: Hold it, my lord! I have served you ever since I was a child, but I have never done you a greater service than now when I ask you to stop.

REGAN: What do you mean, you dog?

FIRST SERVANT: If you were a man, I'd attack you over this matter! How dare you!

CORNWALL: You villain!
[They draw swords and fight; Cornwall is wounded]

FIRST SERVANT: Well, then, come on and take a chance against my anger.

REGAN: Give me thy sword. A peasant stand up thus!
                    [Takes a sword, and runs at him behind]

FIRST SERVANT: O, I am slain! My lord, you have one eye left
    To see some mischief on him. O!   *[Dies]*

CORNWALL: Lest it see more, prevent it. Out, vile jelly!
90   Where is thy lustre now?

GLOUCESTER: All dark and comfortless. Where's my son Edmund?
    Edmund, enkindle all the sparks of nature,
    To quit this horrid act.

REGAN: Out, treacherous villain!
95   Thou call'st on him that hates thee: it was he
    That made the overture of thy treasons to us;
    Who is too good to pity thee.

GLOUCESTER: O my follies! then Edgar was abused.
    Kind gods, forgive me that, and prosper him!

100 REGAN: Go thrust him out at gates, and let him smell
    His way to Dover.   *[Exit one with Gloucester]*
    How is't, my lord? how look you?

CORNWALL: I have received a hurt: follow me, lady.
    Turn out that eyeless villain; throw this slave
105   Upon the dunghill. Regan, I bleed apace:
    Untimely comes this hurt: give me your arm.
                            [Exit Cornwall, led by Regan]

SECOND SERVANT: I'll never care what wickedness I do,
    If this man come to good.

REGAN: *Give me your sword. A peasant standing up like this!*

[Regan takes a sword and runs at him from behind. She kills him]

FIRST SERVANT: *Oh, I've been killed!* [To Gloucester] *My lord, you have one eye left to see that some harm will be done to him! Oh!*   [He dies]

CORNWALL: *Let's prevent that it can see any more. Out, you horrid jelly! Where is your sparkle now?*

GLOUCESTER: *All is dark and there's no comfort! Where's my son Edmund? Edmund, remember your filial affection and avenge this horrid act.*

REGAN: *Go away, you treacherous villain! You call on the one who hates you! He disclosed your treason to us. He's too loyal to pity you.*

GLOUCESTER: *Oh, my foolishness! Then Edgar was wronged. Kind gods, forgive me and support him.*

REGAN: *Go and throw him out of the gates. Let him smell his way to Dover.*   [One Servant exits with Gloucester]
How are you my lord? How are you feeling?

CORNWALL: *I have received a wound. Follow me, lady.* [To Servants] *Throw out this eyeless villain! Throw this slave* (The Servant who died defending Gloucester) *on the dunghill! Regan, I'm bleeding a great deal. This injury comes at a bad time. Give me your arm.*   [Cornwall exits, let by Regan]

SECOND SERVANT: *I don't care what evil things I'll do if this man succeeds.*

THIRD SERVANT: If she live long,
110   And in the end meet the old course of death,
         Women will all turn monsters.

SECOND SERVANT: Let's follow the old earl, and get the Bedlam
         To lead him where he would: his roguish madness
         Allows itself to any thing.

115 THIRD SERVANT: Go thou: I'll fetch some flax and whites of eggs
         To apply to his bleeding face. Now, heaven help him!

[Exeunt severally]

THIRD SERVANT: *If she lives for long and then dies of natural causes, all women will turn into monsters.*

SECOND SERVANT: *Let's follow the old earl and get the crazy beggar to lead him wherever he wants to go. In his madness, he'll do anything we ask him to do.*

THIRD SERVANT: *You go. I'll get some flax and egg whites to apply to his bleeding face. [To alleviate the pain] Now, heaven help him.*

[They exit separately]

like the power w/ his daughters for which he is losing his mind over

↓

social order is being flipped: young hurting old
↓
old hurting young etc.

King Lear questioning social order

ACT IV

SCENE I

The heath.

[Enter Edgar]

EDGAR: Yet better thus, and known to be contemn'd,
    Than still contemn'd and flatter'd. To be worst,
    The lowest and most dejected thing of fortune,
    Stands still in esperance, lives not in fear:
5   The lamentable change is from the best;
    The worst returns to laughter. Welcome, then,
    Thou unsubstantial air that I embrace!
    The wretch that thou hast blown unto the worst
    Owes nothing to thy blasts. But who comes here?

[Enter Gloucester, led by an Old Man]
10   My father, poorly led? World, world, O world!
    But that thy strange mutations make us hate thee,
    Life would not yield to age.

OLD MAN: O, my good lord, I have been your tenant, and your
    father's tenant, these fourscore years.

15 GLOUCESTER: Away, get thee away; good friend, be gone:
    Thy comforts can do me no good at all;
    Thee they may hurt.

ACT IV

SCENE I

The heath.

[EDGAR *enters*]

EDGAR: *It's better to be as I am, openly despised, than to be despised, but treated with false flattery. The lowest thing, rejected by fortune, always lives in hope, and not in fear. The most difficult change is from good to bad. Any change from the worst is for the better. Welcome, then, you tender elements of nature; I embrace you! This wretched man, whom you have blown into torment owes you no thanks. But who comes here?*

[Gloucester enters, led by an Old Man]
My father, guided inadequately? World, world, oh world! If the strange changes of fortune didn't make us hate life, we would not submit to growing old.

OLD MAN: *Oh, my good lord. I have been your tenant, and your father's tenant, for the past eighty years.*

GLOUCESTER: *Go away, go away! Good friend, go away. Your attempts to help me won't do me any good, and they may hurt you.*

OLD MAN: Alack, sir, you cannot see your way.

GLOUCESTER: I have no way, and therefore want no eyes;
20   I stumbled when I saw: full oft 'tis seen,
        Our means secure us, and our mere defects
        Prove our commodities. O dear son Edgar,
        The food of thy abused father's wrath!
        Might I but live to see thee in my touch,
25   I'd say I had eyes again!

OLD MAN: How now! Who's there?

EDGAR: [Aside] O gods! Who is't can say 'I am at the worst'?
       I am worse than e'er I was.

OLD MAN: 'Tis poor mad Tom.

30   EDGAR: [Aside] And worse I may be yet: the worst is not
             So long as we can say 'This is the worst.'

OLD MAN: Fellow, where goest?

GLOUCESTER: Is it a beggar-man?

OLD MAN: Madman and beggar too.

35   GLOUCESTER: He has some reason, else he could not beg.
            I' the last night's storm I such a fellow saw;
            Which made me think a man a worm: my son
            Came then into my mind; and yet my mind
            Was then scarce friends with him: I have heard more since.
40   As flies to wanton boys, are we to the gods.
            They kill us for their sport.

EDGAR: [Aside] How should this be?
       Bad is the trade that must play fool to sorrow,
       Angering itself and others.—Bless thee, master!

OLD MAN: *Alas, sir, you cannot see where you're going.*

GLOUCESTER: *I have no destination, and, therefore, need no eyes. I stumbled when I could see. Too often, prosperity makes us careless, and our defects turn out to be beneficial. Ah, my dear son Edgar, product of your wronged father's anger. If I could live to see you by touching you once more, I'd say I had eyes again.*

OLD MAN: *Hello. Who's there?*

EDGAR: *[Aside] Oh gods! Who was I to say, "I am at the bottom"? I am now worse off than ever before.*

OLD MAN: *It's poor mad Tom.*

EDGAR: *[Aside] And I may yet get worse. The worst hasn't happened as long as we can say, "This is the worst."*

OLD MAN: *Fellow, where are you going?*

GLOUCESTER: *Is it a beggar?*

OLD MAN: *A madman, and beggar, too.*

GLOUCESTER: *He has some sanity, otherwise he wouldn't be able to beg. Last night in the storm, I saw a fellow like him. He made me think of men as insignificant and low. Then, my son came into my mind, though, at the time, I had no friendly thought for him. I have learned more since then. We are to the gods what flies are to playful boys. They kill us for fun.*

EDGAR: *[Aside] How can this be? It's a bad situation when you must disguise your sadness and pretend to be foolish. It torments everybody. [To Gloucester] God bless you, master.*

185

45 GLOUCESTER: Is that the naked fellow?

OLD MAN: Ay, my lord.

GLOUCESTER: Then, prithee, get thee gone: if, for my sake,
      Thou wilt o'ertake us, hence a mile or twain,
      I' the way toward Dover, do it for ancient love;
50   And bring some covering for this naked soul,
      Who I'll entreat to lead me.

OLD MAN: Alack, sir, he is mad.

GLOUCESTER: 'Tis the times' plague, when madmen lead the blind.
      Do as I bid thee, or rather do thy pleasure;
55   Above the rest, be gone.

OLD MAN: I'll bring him the best 'parel that I have,
      Come on't what will.   *[Exit]*

GLOUCESTER: Sirrah, naked fellow,—

EDGAR: Poor Tom's a-cold. *[Aside]* I cannot daub it further.

60 GLOUCESTER: Come hither, fellow.

EDGAR: *[Aside]* And yet I must.—Bless thy sweet eyes, they bleed.

GLOUCESTER: Know'st thou the way to Dover?

EDGAR: Both stile and gate, horse-way and foot-path. Poor Tom hath
      been scared out of his good wits: bless thee, good man's son,
65   from the foul fiend! five fiends have been in poor Tom at once;
      of lust, as Obidicut; Hobbididence, prince of dumbness; Mahu,
      of stealing; Modo, of murder; Flibbertigibbet, of mopping and

186

GLOUCESTER: Is this the naked fool?

OLD MAN: Yes, my lord.

GLOUCESTER: Then, please, leave. If, for my sake, you want to meet up with us a mile or two from here, do it for the sake of your former alliance with me. And bring some clothes for this naked creature, whom I will ask to guide me.

OLD MAN: But sir, he's mad.

GLOUCESTER: Our times are evil, when madmen lead the blind. Do as I've asked you to do. Or do whatever you want to do. Above all, go away.

OLD MAN: I'll bring him the best outfit that I own, no matter what happens.   [He exits]

GLOUCESTER: Hello, naked fellow.

EDGAR: Poor Tom's cold! [Aside] I cannot continue with this disguise any longer.

GLOUCESTER: Come here, fellow.

EDGAR: [Aside] And yet, I must. God bless your sweet eyes. They bleed.

GLOUCESTER: Do you know the way to Dover?

EDGAR: By horse path or footpath. Poor Tom has been scared out of his wits. Bless you, good man, from the foul fiend. Five fiends have been inside poor Tom all at once: Obidicut, the fiend of lust; Hobbididence, the prince of dumbness; Mahu, the fiend of stealing;

mowing, who since possesses chambermaids and waiting-wom-
en. So, bless thee, master!

70 GLOUCESTER: Here, take this purse, thou whom the heavens' plagues
    Have humbled to all strokes: that I am wretched
    Makes thee the happier: heavens, deal so still!
    Let the superfluous and lust-dieted man,
    That slaves your ordinance, that will not see
75   Because he doth not feel, feel your power quickly;
    So distribution should undo excess,
    And each man have enough. Dost thou know Dover?

EDGAR: Ay, master.

GLOUCESTER: There is a cliff, whose high and bending head
80   Looks fearfully in the confined deep:
    Bring me but to the very brim of it,
    And I'll repair the misery thou dost bear
    With something rich about me: from that place
    I shall no leading need.

85 EDGAR: Give me thy arm:
    Poor Tom shall lead thee.

                              [Exeunt]

Modo, the fiend of murder; and Flibbertigibbbet, the fiend of grimaces, who has moved on to possess chambermaids and servant women. So, bless you, master.

GLOUCESTER: Here, take this purse! You, who's been reduced to bear all this misfortune. My wretchedness shall make you less wretched! Heavens, let it be that way! Let any man who has more than he needs and over-indulges, who considers your needs inferior to his own desires, who doesn't want to see things he doesn't have to feel himself, quickly experience your power. The excess of wealth shall be distributed so that every man has enough Do you know Dover?

EDGAR: Yes, master.

GLOUCESTER: There is a high and overhanging cliff that fearfully looks into the Straits of Dover. Lead me just to the edge of that cliff, and I'll remedy the misery you endure with something valuable I have on me. From that place on, I won't need any guidance.

EDGAR: Give me your arm. Poor Tom will lead you.

[They exit]

SCENE II

Before Albany's palace.

[Enter Goneril and Edmund]

GONERIL: Welcome, my lord: I marvel our mild husband
    Not met us on the way.

[Enter Oswald[
            Now, where's your master'?

OSWALD: Madam, within; but never man so changed.
5   I told him of the army that was landed;
    He smiled at it: I told him you were coming:
    His answer was 'The worse:' of Gloucester's treachery,
    And of the loyal service of his son,
    When I inform'd him, then he call'd me sot,
10   And told me I had turn'd the wrong side out:
    What most he should dislike seems pleasant to him;
    What like, offensive.

GONERIL: *[To Edmund]* Then shall you go no further.
    It is the cowish terror of his spirit,
15   That dares not undertake: he'll not feel wrongs
    Which tie him to an answer. Our wishes on the way
    May prove effects. Back, Edmund, to my brother;
    Hasten his musters and conduct his powers:
    I must change arms at home, and give the distaff
20   Into my husband's hands. This trusty servant
    Shall pass between us: ere long you are like to hear,
    If you dare venture in your own behalf,
    A mistress's command. Wear this; spare speech;
                           [Giving a favour]
    Decline your head: this kiss, if it durst speak,
25   Would stretch thy spirits up into the air:
    Conceive, and fare thee well.

SCENE II

Before the Duke of Albany's palace.

[Goneril and Edmund enter]

GONERIL: *Welcome, my lord. I wonder why my gentle husband has not met us halfway.*

[Oswald enters]
Now, where's your master?

OSWALD: *Inside, madam. But no man has ever changed like he has. I told him about the army that has arrived. He smiled at it. I told you were coming, and his answer was, "That's worse!" When I informed him of Gloucester's treachery and of his son's loyal services, he called me "fool," and told me I have completely reversed the facts. What he should dislike most, appears to please him. Things he should like, appear to offend him.*

GONERIL: [To Edmund] *In that case, you should go no further. It's his cowardly disposition that doesn't dare to take responsibility. He won't respond to any insults that demand action. The hopes we talked over on the way here must be realized. Return to my brother-in-law, Edmund. Speed up the assembling of his troops and lead his army. I must take matters into my hands like a man would and let my husband act like a woman instead. This trusted servant will exchange our communications. Before long, you're likely to hear a further command from your mistress—if you dare to act selfishly. Wear this; don't say anything.* [Handing him a gift] *Lower your head. This kiss, if it could speak, would invigorate you. Think about the possibilities. Good bye.*

EDMUND: Yours in the ranks of death.

GONERIL: My most dear Gloucester!

                                        [Exit Edmund]

      O, the difference of man and man!

30   To thee a woman's services are due:

      My fool usurps my body.

OSWALD: Madam, here comes my lord.

                                        [Exit]

[Enter Albany]

GONERIL: I have been worth the whistle.

ALBANY: O Goneril!

35   You are not worth the dust which the rude wind

      Blows in your face. I fear your disposition:

      That nature, which contemns its origin,

      Cannot be border'd certain in itself;

      She that herself will sliver and disbranch

40   From her material sap, perforce must wither

      And come to deadly use.

GONERIL: No more; the text is foolish.

ALBANY: Wisdom and goodness to the vile seem vile:

      Filths savour but themselves. What have you done?

45   Tigers, not daughters, what have you perform'd?

      A father, and a gracious aged man,

      Whose reverence even the head-lugg'd bear would lick,

      Most barbarous, most degenerate! have you madded.

      Could my good brother suffer you to do it?

50   A man, a prince, by him so benefited!

      If that the heavens do not their visible spirits

      Send quickly down to tame these vile offences,

      It will come,

EDMUND: *Yours till the day I die.*

GONERIL: *My dearest Gloucester!* [To Edmund].

[Edmund exits.]
Oh, the difference between one man and another. You deserve the services of a woman! My fool receives my body.

OSWALD: *Madam, here comes my lord.*

[He exits. Albany enters]

GONERIL: *I should have been worth your trouble to come and meet me on my way!*

ALBANY: *Oh Goneril! You're not worth the dust the rude wind blows into your face! I fear your temperament. A creature that spurns its father cannot be kept under control safely. Any woman who cuts herself off from her source of nourishment must wither and find her destruction.*

GONERIL: *No more of this! You speak foolishly.*

ALBANY: *Wisdom and goodness seem repulsive to the repulsive creature. To the filthy, everything seems filthy. What have you done, acting like tigers, not daughters? What have you done! A father, and a gracious, aged man, who would be respected even by an infuriated, captive bear, has been driven to madness in the most barbarous, degenerate manner! Did my good brother-in-law allow you to do this? A man, a prince, who received so many benefits from him! If the gods do not quickly send their spirits down to stop these evil insults, then humans will inevitably devour each other, like monsters of the deep sea.*

Humanity must perforce prey on itself,
55 Like monsters of the deep.

GONERIL: Milk-liver'd man!
That bear'st a cheek for blows, a head for wrongs;
Who hast not in thy brows an eye discerning
Thine honour from thy suffering; that not know'st
60 Fools do those villains pity who are punish'd
Ere they have done their mischief. Where's thy drum?
France spreads his banners in our noiseless land;
With plumed helm thy slayer begins threats;
Whiles thou, a moral fool, sit'st still, and criest
65 'Alack, why does he so?'

ALBANY: See thyself, devil!
Proper deformity seems not in the fiend
So horrid as in woman.

GONERIL: O vain fool!

70 ALBANY: Thou changed and self-cover'd thing, for shame,
Be-monster not thy feature. Were't my fitness
To let these hands obey my blood,
They are apt enough to dislocate and tear
Thy flesh and bones: howe'er thou art a fiend,
75 A woman's shape doth shield thee.

GONERIL: Marry, your manhood now—

[Enter a Messenger]

ALBANY: What news?

MESSENGER: O, my good lord, the Duke of Cornwall's dead:
Slain by his servant, going to put out
80 The other eye of Gloucester.

194

GONERIL: *Cowardly man! Your face is asking to be hit, and your mind is asking to be insulted. You don't have an eye for detecting what should be tolerated and what should be resented. You don't know that only fools feel pity for villains who are punished before they have been able to commit their crime. Where are your military drums? The king of France announces his presence in our unprepared country and begins to threaten your country with his military show, while you, a moralizing fool, sit here and cry, "Alas, why does he do this?"*

ALBANY: *Look at yourself, you devil! Deformity seems more horrible in a woman than in the devil himself.*

GONERIL: *Oh, useless fool!*

ALBANY: *You changed and deceitful monster! For shame, don't make yourself look even more hideous! If it were proper for me to let these hands act upon their impulses, I would be inclined to tear apart your flesh and bones. Although you are a fiend, your female form protects you.*

GONERIL: *Your manhood! Ha!*

[A messenger enters]

ALBANY: *What news do you bring?*

MESSENGER: *Oh, my good lord, the Duke of Cornwall is dead, murdered by his servant, as he was trying to put out Gloucester's second eye.*

ALBANY: Gloucester's eye!

MESSENGER: A servant that he bred, thrill'd with remorse,
        Opposed against the act, bending his sword
        To his great master; who, thereat enraged,
85   Flew on him, and amongst them fell'd him dead;
        But not without that harmful stroke, which since
        Hath pluck'd him after.

ALBANY: This shows you are above,
        You justicers, that these our nether crimes
90   So speedily can venge! But, O poor Gloucester!
        Lost he his other eye?

MESSENGER: Both, both, my lord.
        This letter, madam, craves a speedy answer;
        'Tis from your sister.

95   GONERIL: [Aside] One way I like this well;
        But being widow, and my Gloucester with her,
        May all the building in my fancy pluck
        Upon my hateful life: another way,
        The news is not so tart.—I'll read, and answer.
                                        [Exit]

100 ALBANY: Where was his son when they did take his eyes?

MESSENGER: Come with my lady hither.

ALBANY: He is not here.

MESSENGER: No, my good lord; I met him back again.

ALBANY: Knows he the wickedness?

105 MESSENGER: Ay, my good lord; 'twas he inform'd against him;

196

ALBANY: *Gloucester's eyes?*

MESSENGER: *A servant he had trained, filled with pity, tried to defend him and raised his sword against his master. He became enraged, attacked him and, together with the others, killed him, but not before the duke received that harmful blow which has now taken his life.*

ALBANY: *This proves that your are watching above, oh heavenly judges, who can avenge our crimes on earth so quickly! But, oh, poor Gloucester! Did he lose his other eye?*

MESSENGER: *Both, both, my lord.* [To Goneril] *This letter, madam, demands a quick answer. It's from your sister.*

GONERIL: [Aside] *In one way, I am glad. But Regan being a widow, and my Gloucester being with her, could ruin everything I have imagined for my future. In other ways, these news are not so bad. I'll read the letter and answer it.*

[She exits]

ALBANY: *Where was his son when they blinded him?*

MESSENGER: *On his way here with my lady.*

ALBANY: *He's not here.*

MESSENGER: *No, my good lord. I met him on his way back.*

ALBANY: *Does he know about the evil deed?*

MESSENGER: *Yes, my good lord. It was he who discovered his father, and*

And quit the house on purpose, that their punishment
Might have the freer course.

ALBANY: Gloucester, I live
        To thank thee for the love thou show'dst the king,
110   And to revenge thine eyes. Come hither, friend:
        Tell me what more thou know'st.

                                        [Exeunt]

[handwritten notes:]
· the more power Goneril gains the more
  she disregards others deeper + deeper : kingdm +
                                              army
· characters in power are beginning
  to face division ·

SCENE III

The French camp near Dover.

[Enter Kent and a Gentleman]

KENT: Why the King of France is so suddenly gone back know you
    the reason?

GENTLEMAN: Something he left imperfect in the state, which since
    his coming forth is thought of; which imports to the kingdom
5   so much fear and danger, that his personal return was most
    required and necessary.

KENT: Who hath he left behind him general?

GENTLEMAN: The Marshal of France, Monsieur La Far.

KENT: Did your letters pierce the queen to any demonstration of
10   grief?

GENTLEMAN: Ay, sir; she took them, read them in my presence;
    And now and then an ample tear trill'd down
    Her delicate cheek: it seem'd she was a queen
    Over her passion; who, most rebel-like,
15   Sought to be king o'er her.

198

he left the house on purpose, so that they could have a free hand with their punishment.

ALBANY: *Gloucester, I live to thank you for the love you have shown to the king and to avenge your eyes. Come here, friend, tell me what else you know.*

[They exit]

SCENE III

The French camp near Dover.

[Kent and a Gentleman enter]

KENT: *Do you know why the king of France has so suddenly returned home?*

GENTLEMAN: *After coming here, he remembered some unfinished business in his country, which caused so much fear and danger in his kingdom that his personal return was necessary.*

KENT: *Who has he left behind as the General in charge?*

GENTLEMAN: *The Marshal of France, Monsieur La Far.*

KENT: *Did your letters move the queen to any signs of grief?*

GENTLEMAN: *Yes, sir. She took them and read them in my presence, and, every now and then, a large tear trickled down her delicate cheek. Like a queen, she controlled her emotions, but they, like rebels, tried to overpower her.*

KENT: O, then it moved her.

GENTLEMAN: Not to a rage: patience and sorrow strove
     Who should express her goodliest. You have seen
     Sunshine and rain at once: her smiles and tears
20   Were like a better way: those happy smilets,
     That play'd on her ripe lip, seem'd not to know
     What guests were in her eyes; which parted thence,
     As pearls from diamonds dropp'd. In brief,
     Sorrow would be a rarity most beloved,
25   If all could so become it.

KENT: Made she no verbal question?

GENTLEMAN: 'Faith, once or twice she heaved the name of 'father'
     Pantingly forth, as if it press'd her heart:
     Cried 'Sisters! sisters! Shame of ladies! sisters!
30   Kent! father! sisters! What, i' the storm? i' the night?
     Let pity not be believed!' There she shook
     The holy water from her heavenly eyes,
     And clamour moisten'd: then away she started
     To deal with grief alone.

35 KENT: It is the stars,
     The stars above us, govern our conditions;
     Else one self mate and mate could not beget
     Such different issues. You spoke not with her since?

GENTLEMAN: No.

40 KENT: Was this before the king return'd?

GENTLEMAN: No, since.

KENT: Well, sir, the poor distressed Lear's i' the town;
     Who sometime, in his better tune, remembers
     What we are come about, and by no means
45   Will yield to see his daughter.

KENT: *Oh, then she was moved.*

GENTLEMAN: *Not into a violent outburst. Endurance and sorrow fought over who might portray her best. You have seen sunshine and rain at the same time? Her smiles and tears were similar. Those happy little smiles that played on her red lips didn't seem to know about the tears in her eyes, which fell like pearls dropping from diamonds. In short, sorrow would be precious if everybody could bear it so gracefully.*

KENT: *Didn't she say anything?*

GENTLEMAN: *Truly, once or twice, she breathed the name "father," as if it crushed her heart. She cried, "Sisters, sisters! Shameful ladies! Sisters! Kent, father, sisters! What, in the storm? At night? Oh pity, it's impossible to believe!" Then genuine tears fell from her heavenly eyes, and she was overpowered by her feelings. Then she left in order to deal with her grief in private.*

KENT: *The stars above us that determine our personalities; otherwise one and the same, husband and wife could not beget such different children. You have not spoken to her since?*

GENTLEMAN: *Not since then.*

KENT: *Was this before the king returned?*

GENTLEMAN: *No.*

KENT: *Well, sir, the poor, distressed Lear is in town. Sometimes, in his saner moments, he remembers why we came here, and he will, by no means, consent to see his daughter.*

GENTLEMAN: Why, good sir?

KENT: A sovereign shame so elbows him: his own unkindness,
        That stripp'd her from his benediction, turn'd her
        To foreign casualties, gave her dear rights
50   To his dog-hearted daughters, these things sting
        His mind so venomously, that burning shame
        Detains him from Cordelia.

GENTLEMAN: Alack, poor gentleman!

KENT: Of Albany's and Cornwall's powers you heard not?

55 GENTLEMAN: 'Tis so, they are afoot.

KENT: Well, sir, I'll bring you to our master Lear,
      And leave you to attend him: some dear cause
      Will in concealment wrap me up awhile;
      When I am known aright, you shall not grieve
60   Lending me this acquaintance. I pray you, go
      Along with me.
                                        [Exeunt]

GENTLEMAN: Why, good sir?

KENT: An overpowering shame keeps him away. His own unkindness—which took away his blessings from her, gave her over to an uncertain life abroad, gave her share to his hard-hearted daughters—plagues his conscience so bitterly, that the burning shame keeps him away from Cordelia.

GENTLEMAN: Alas, poor gentleman!

KENT: You haven't heard anything about the armies of Albany and Cornwall?

GENTLEMAN: It's true. They're on their way.

KENT: Well, sir, I'll bring you to our master Lear and leave you to take care of him. Some important reason will force me into hiding for a while. When I can reveal who I am, you will not regret giving me your assistance. Please, come with me.

[They exit]

SCENE IV

The same. A tent.

[Enter, with drum and colours, Cordelia, Doctor, and Soldiers]

CORDELIA: Alack, 'tis he: why, he was met even now
    As mad as the vex'd sea; singing aloud;
    Crown'd with rank fumiter and furrow-weeds,
    With bur-docks, hemlock, nettles, cuckoo-flowers,
5   Darnel, and all the idle weeds that grow
    In our sustaining corn. A century send forth;
    Search every acre in the high-grown field,
    And bring him to our eye.   *[Exit an Officer]*
    What can man's wisdom
10   In the restoring his bereaved sense?
    He that helps him take all my outward worth.

DOCTOR: There is means, madam:
    Our foster-nurse of nature is repose,
    The which he lacks; that to provoke in him,
15   Are many simples operative, whose power
    Will close the eye of anguish.

CORDELIA: All blest secrets,
    All you unpublish'd virtues of the earth,
    Spring with my tears! be aidant and remediate
20   In the good man's distress! Seek, seek for him;
    Lest his ungovern'd rage dissolve the life
    That wants the means to lead it.

[Enter a Messenger]

MESSENGER: News, madam;
    The British powers are marching hitherward.

SCENE IV

A Tent.

[Cordelia, a Doctor, and Soldiers enter. Drums sound]

CORDELIA: *Alas, it's him! He was seen just now, as mad as the disturbed sea, singing loudly, wearing a crown made from fumitory herbs and other weeds—burdock, hemlock, nettles, cuckoo-flowers, grass— and all the common weeds that grow in our life-sustaining wheat. Send a hundred soldiers to search every acre of the high-grown field, and bring him into our sight!*

[An officer exits]

What can human knowledge do to restore his lost mind? Whoever helps him will receive all my worldly possessions!

DOCTOR: *There is a way, madam. The healing mechanism of our nature is rest, which he lacks. In order to induce sleep, there are many effective medicinal herbs that will soothe his pain.*

CORDELIA: *All you beneficial herbs on this earth, though unknown, grow as my tears flow. Be helpful and remedial to the good man's distress! Look, look for him, or his uncontrolled frenzy will cause the end of his life that lacks reason.*

[A messenger enters]

MESSENGER: *News, madam. The British army is approaching.*

25 CORDELIA: 'Tis known before; our preparation stands
　　　　　In expectation of them. O dear father,
　　　　　It is thy business that I go about;
　　　　　Therefore great France
　　　　　My mourning and important tears hath pitied.
30　　　　No blown ambition doth our arms incite,
　　　　　But love, dear love, and our aged father's right:
　　　　　Soon may I hear and see him!

　　　　　　　　　　　　　　　　　　　　　　[Exeunt]

·cordelia's presence is that of sunshine
as it is going to help her earlier but tears of raindas
her path is authentic.

SCENE V

Gloucester's castle.

[Enter Regan and Oswald]

REGAN: But are my brother's powers set forth?

OSWALD:　　　　　　　　Ay, madam.

REGAN: Himself in person there?

OSWALD:　　　　　　　Madam, with much ado:
5　　　Your sister is the better soldier.

REGAN: Lord Edmund spake not with your lord at home?

OSWALD: No, madam.

REGAN: What might import my sister's letter to him?

OSWALD: I know not, lady.

CORDELIA: *We knew that was coming. Our deployed troops are expecting them. Oh, dear father. I am pursuing your interests. That's why the great king of France has pardoned my grief and my persistent tears. No swollen ambition provokes us to declare war, but love, dear love, and the rights of our aged father. May I soon hear him and see him!*

[They exit]

SCENE V

Gloucester's castle.

[Regan and Oswald enter]

REGAN: *Have my brother-in-law's troops set out?*

OSWALD: *Yes, madam.*

REGAN: *Is he himself there, in person?*

OSWALD: *Madam, after much persuasion. Your sister is the better soldier.*

REGAN: *Lord Edmund did not speak with your lord at his house?*

OSWALD: *I don't know, madam.*

REGAN: *What might sister's letter say to him?*

OSWALD: *I don't know, my lady.*

10 REGAN: Faith, he is posted hence on serious matter.
It was great ignorance, Gloucester's eyes being out,
To let him live: where he arrives he moves
All hearts against us: Edmund, I think, is gone,
In pity of his misery, to dispatch
15 His nighted life: moreover, to descry
The strength o' the enemy.

OSWALD: I must needs after him, madam, with my letter.

REGAN: Our troops set forth to-morrow: stay with us;
The ways are dangerous.

20 OSWALD: I may not, madam:
My lady charged my duty in this business.

REGAN: Why should she write to Edmund? Might not you
Transport her purposes by word? Belike,
Something—I know not what: I'll love thee much,
25 Let me unseal the letter.

OSWALD: Madam, I had rather—

REGAN: I know your lady does not love her husband;
I am sure of that: and at her late being here
She gave strange oeillades and most speaking looks
30 To noble Edmund. I know you are of her bosom.

OSWALD: I, madam?

REGAN: I speak in understanding; you are; I know't:
Therefore I do advise you, take this note:
My lord is dead; Edmund and I have talk'd;
35 And more convenient is he for my hand
Than for your lady's: you may gather more.
If you do find him, pray you, give him this;

REGAN: Truly, he has ridden off hastily on serious business. It was very foolish to let Gloucester live after he was blinded. Wherever he goes, he turns people's hearts against us. I think Edmund has left to put an end to his father's life in darkness, because he was moved to pity by his misery. Moreover, he will determine the strength of the enemy's army.

OSWALD: I must follow him with my letter, madam.

REGAN: Our troops set out tomorrow. Stay with us. The roads are dangerous.

OSWALD: I can't, madam. My lady commanded strict obedience in this matter.

REGAN: Why should she write to Edmund? Could you not deliver her message by word of mouth? Perhaps—something—I don't know what—I'll make it worth your while if you let me open the letter.

OSWALD: Madam, I'd rather—

REGAN: I know your lady doesn't love her husband. I am sure of that. And when she was here recently, she threw strange amorous glances and meaningful looks to noble Edmund. I know you are in her confidence.

OSWALD: I, madam?

REGAN: I know what I'm saying: you are. I know it! Therefore, I advise you to take note of what I'll say. My lord is dead. Edmund and I have talked; he is more suitable for me than for your lady. You can draw your own conclusions. If you find him, please give this to him. And if your mistress hears your report of what I have said, please ask her to think reasonably. So, goodbye. I

And when your mistress hears thus much from you,
I pray, desire her call her wisdom to her.
40 So, fare you well.
If you do chance to hear of that blind traitor,
Preferment falls on him that cuts him off.

OSWALD: Would I could meet him, madam! I should show
What party I do follow.

45 REGAN: Fare thee well.

                                    [Exeunt]

SCENE VI

Fields near Dover.

[Enter Gloucester, and Edgar dressed like a peasant]

GLOUCESTER: When shall we come to the top of that same hill?

EDGAR: You do climb up it now: look, how we labour.

GLOUCESTER: Methinks the ground is even.

EDGAR: Horrible steep.
5   Hark, do you hear the sea?

GLOUCESTER: No, truly.

EDGAR: Why, then, your other senses grow imperfect
By your eyes' anguish.

you happen to hear about the blind traitor, whoever kills him will be rewarded.

Oswald: *I wish I'd meet him, madam. I could show whose side I'm on.*

Regan: *Farewell.*

[They exit]

SCENE VI

Fields near Dover.

[Gloucester, and Edgar, dressed like a peasant, enter]

Gloucester: *When will we reach the top of the hill?*

Edgar: *You're climbing up right now. Look, how we struggle!*

Gloucester: *The ground feels even to me.*

Edgar: *It's horribly steep. Listen. Do you hear the sea?*

Gloucester: *No, honestly.*

Edgar: *Well, then your other senses are fading due to the pain in your eyes.*

211

GLOUCESTER: So may it be, indeed:
10   Methinks thy voice is alter'd; and thou speak'st
    In better phrase and matter than thou didst.

EDGAR: You're much deceived: in nothing am I changed
    But in my garments.

GLOUCESTER: Methinks you're better spoken.

15 EDGAR: Come on, sir; here's the place: stand still. How fearful
    And dizzy 'tis, to cast one's eyes so low!
    The crows and choughs that wing the midway air
    Show scarce so gross as beetles: half way down
    Hangs one that gathers samphire, dreadful trade!
20   Methinks he seems no bigger than his head:
    The fishermen, that walk upon the beach,
    Appear like mice; and yond tall anchoring bark,
    Diminish'd to her cock; her cock, a buoy
    Almost too small for sight: the murmuring surge,
25   That on the unnumber'd idle pebbles chafes,
    Cannot be heard so high. I'll look no more;
    Lest my brain turn, and the deficient sight
    Topple down headlong.

GLOUCESTER: Set me where you stand.

30 EDGAR: Give me your hand: you are now within a foot
    Of the extreme verge: for all beneath the moon
    Would I not leap upright.

GLOUCESTER: Let go my hand.
    Here, friend, 's another purse; in it a jewel
35   Well worth a poor man's taking: fairies and gods
    Prosper it with thee! Go thou farther off;
    Bid me farewell, and let me hear thee going.

EDGAR: Now fare you well, good sir.

GLOUCESTER: *That may indeed be the case. I feel like your voice has changed, and you speak more coherently than you used to.*

EDGAR: *You're very wrong. Nothing has changed about me, except for my clothes.*

GLOUCESTER: *I feel like you speak more clearly now.*

EDGAR: *Come on, sir. Here's the place. Stand still. It makes me frightened and dizzy to look all the way down! The crows and jackdaws that are flying halfway down look hardly as large as beetles. Halfway down, there's someone gathering herbs. What a dreadful job! He seems to be no bigger than his head! The fishermen who walk along the beach look like mice. And over there, the large vessel at anchor, is reduced to the size of a rowingboat, and the rowing boar looks like a buoy, almost too small to be seen. The murmuring waves that wash over the countless, useless pebbles, cannot be heard so high above. I won't look anymore, or I'll become dizzy, lose my sight, and fall headlong over the cliff.*

GLOUCESTER: *Set me where you stand.*

EDGAR: *Give me your hand. You are now within a foot of the extreme edge. Not for anything in the world would I jump up and down!*

GLOUCESTER: *Let go off my hand. Here, my friend, is another purse. Inside is a jewel that's worth a lot to a poor man. May fairies and gods multiply your wealth. Go further away. Say goodbye, and let me hear you walk away.*

EDGAR: *Farewell, good sir.*

213

GLOUCESTER: With all my heart.

40   EDGAR: Why I do trifle thus with his despair
        Is done to cure it.

GLOUCESTER: *[Kneeling]* O you mighty gods!
        This world I do renounce, and, in your sights,
        Shake patiently my great affliction off:
45   If I could bear it longer, and not fall
        To quarrel with your great opposeless wills,
        My snuff and loathed part of nature should
        Burn itself out. If Edgar live, O, bless him!
        Now, fellow, fare thee well.   *[He falls forward]*

50   EDGAR: Gone, sir: farewell.
        And yet I know not how conceit may rob
        The treasury of life, when life itself
        Yields to the theft: had he been where he thought,
        By this, had thought been past. Alive or dead?
55   Ho, you sir! friend! Hear you, sir! speak!
        Thus might he pass indeed: yet he revives.
        What are you, sir?

GLOUCESTER: Away, and let me die.

EDGAR: Hadst thou been aught but gossamer, feathers, air,
60   So many fathom down precipitating,
        Thou'dst shiver'd like an egg: but thou dost breathe;
        Hast heavy substance; bleed'st not; speak'st; art sound.
        Ten masts at each make not the altitude
        Which thou hast perpendicularly fell:
65   Thy life's a miracle. Speak yet again.

GLOUCESTER: But have I fall'n, or no?

EDGAR: From the dread summit of this chalky bourn.
        Look up a-height; the shrill-gorged lark so far
        Cannot be seen or heard: do but look up.

GLOUCESTER: *With all my heart.*

EDGAR: *I'm going along with his misery only to cure it.*

GLOUCESTER: *[Kneeling] Oh, you mighty gods. I renounce this world, and, in your sight, I patiently shake off my suffering. If I could bear it any longer without rebelling against your great will that must not be opposed, the smoldering wick and hated remnant of my life would burn out. If Edgar lives, may the gods bless him! Now, farewell, farewell.*

[He falls forward, attempting to jump off the cliff]

EDGAR: *Gone, sir, farewell! And yet I don't know if imagination only can take his life, if that's what he desires. If he had been where he thought he was, his thoughts would now be gone. Alive or dead? Hello, you, sir! Do you hear, sir? Speak.—He might die like this indeed!.—But he revives! How are you, sir?*

GLOUCESTER: *Go away, and let me die!*

EDGAR: *If you had been anything but gossamer, feathers, or air, you'd have been smashed like an egg, after falling so deep! But you breathe! You are solid. You're not bleeding! You speak, and you're alright! Ten masts tied end to end don't add up to the height you have fallen from. Your life is a miracle! Speak again!*

GLOUCESTER: *Did I fall or not?*

EDGAR: *From the dreadful summit of the chalky cliff. Look up high. The shrill-sounding lark cannot be seen or heard so far away. Do look up.*

70 GLOUCESTER: Alack, I have no eyes.
      Is wretchedness deprived that benefit,
      To end itself by death? 'Twas yet some comfort,
      When misery could beguile the tyrant's rage,
      And frustrate his proud will.

75 EDGAR: Give me your arm:
      Up: so. How is't? Feel you your legs? You stand.

GLOUCESTER: Too well, too well.

EDGAR: This is above all strangeness.
      Upon the crown o' the cliff, what thing was that
80   Which parted from you?

GLOUCESTER: A poor unfortunate beggar.

EDGAR: As I stood here below, methought his eyes
      Were two full moons; he had a thousand noses,
      Horns whelk'd and waved like the enridged sea:
85   It was some fiend; therefore, thou happy father,
      Think that the clearest gods, who make them honours
      Of men's impossibilities, have preserved thee.

GLOUCESTER: I do remember now: henceforth I'll bear
      Affliction till it do cry out itself
90   'Enough, enough,' and die. That thing you speak of,
      I took it for a man; often 'twould say
      'The fiend, the fiend:' he led me to that place.

EDGAR: Bear free and patient thoughts. But who comes here?

[Enter King Lear, fantastically dressed with wild flowers]
      The safer sense will ne'er accommodate
95   His master thus.

216

GLOUCESTER: *Alas, I have no eyes! Is a wretched man deprived of the privilege to end his own life? It was a comfort when misery could cheat the tyrant's anger and defeat his proud will.*

EDGAR: *Give me your arm. Stand up! Like this! How do you feel? Do you feel your legs? You're standing.*

GLOUCESTER: *Too well, too well.*

EDGAR: *This is more than strange. On the top of the cliff, what was this thing creature that left you?*

GLOUCESTER: *A poor, unfortunate beggar.*

EDGAR: *From down here, it looked as if his eyes were two full moons, he had a thousand noses, with horns twisted and intricate like the raging sea. It was a devil. Therefore, fortunate old man, believe that the most righteous gods, who gain our esteem by doing what ordinary men can't do, have saved you.*

GLOUCESTER: *I do remember now. From now on, I'll bear my misery until it decides for itself that I've suffered enough, and then I'll die. That thing you have described, I thought was a man. He often said, "The fiend, the fiend." He led me to that place.*

EDGAR: *Think careless, untroubled thoughts! But who comes here?*

[Lear enters, mad, wearing a crown made of weeds and flowers]
   No one in his right mind would dress himself up like this!

King Lear: No, they cannot touch me for coining; I am the king
    himself.

Edgar: O thou side-piercing sight!

King Lear: Nature's above art in that respect. There's your press-
100   money. That fellow handles his bow like a crow-keeper: draw
    me a clothier's yard. Look, look, a mouse! Peace, peace; this
    piece of toasted cheese will do 't. There's my gauntlet; I'll prove
    it on a giant. Bring up the brown bills. O, well flown, bird! i' the
    clout, i' the clout: hewgh! Give the word.

105   Edgar: Sweet marjoram.

King Lear: Pass.

Gloucester: I know that voice.

King Lear: Ha! Goneril, with a white beard! They flattered me like
    a dog; and told me I had white hairs in my beard ere the black
110   ones were there. To say 'ay' and 'no' to every thing that I said!—
    'Ay' and 'no' too was no good divinity. When the rain came to
    wet me once, and the wind to make me chatter; when the thun-
    der would not peace at my bidding; there I found 'em, there I
    smelt 'em out. Go to, they are not men o' their words: they told
115   me I was every thing; 'tis a lie, I am not ague-proof.

Gloucester: The trick of that voice I do well remember:
    Is 't not the king?

King Lear: Ay, every inch a king:
    When I do stare, see how the subject quakes.
120   I pardon that man's life. What was thy cause? Adultery?

KING LEAR: *No, they cannot censure me for forging coins; I am the king himself!*

EDGAR: *Oh, you heart-wrenching sight!*

KING LEAR: *Nature defeats art in this respect. Here's your money. This boy handles his bow clumsily. Draw the bow out all the way. Look, look, a mouse. Quiet, quiet, this piece of toasted cheese will take care of it. There's my gauntlet! I'll even take on a giant. Bring on the halberdiers! Oh, you've flown well, arrow. Hit the target! Hit the target! Give me the password! [Noticing Edgar]*

madness —

EDGAR: *Sweet marjoram.*

KING LEAR: *Pass.*

GLOUCESTER: *I know that voice.*

KING LEAR: *Ha! Goneril, with a white beard. They flattered me and told me that I was wise when I was but a child. They said "Yes" and "No" to everything I said! "Yes" and "No" is no good basis for theology. When one day, the rain came and soaked me, and the wind made my teeth chatter, and the thunder would not calm down even though I told it to—that's when I found out about them; that's when I smelled them out. See, they are not men who keep their words. They told me I could do anything. It was a lie—I'm not immune to shivering*

GLOUCESTER: *I remember the sound of that voice well. Isn't it the king?*

KING LEAR: *Yes, every inch a king! When I stare at my subjects, see how they tremble. I'll pardon that man's life. What was your offense? Adultery? You shall not die! Die for adultery? No! The*

219

Thou shalt not die: die for adultery! No:
The wren goes to 't, and the small gilded fly
Does lecher in my sight.
Let copulation thrive; for Gloucester's bastard son
125   Was kinder to his father than my daughters
Got 'tween the lawful sheets.
To 't, luxury, pell-mell! for I lack soldiers.
Behold yond simpering dame,
Whose face between her forks presages snow;
130   That minces virtue, and does shake the head
To hear of pleasure's name;
The fitchew, nor the soiled horse, goes to 't
With a more riotous appetite.
Down from the waist they are Centaurs,
135   Though women all above:
But to the girdle do the gods inherit,
Beneath is all the fiends';
There's hell, there's darkness, there's the sulphurous pit,
Burning, scalding, stench, consumption; fie, fie, fie! pah, pah!
140   Give me an ounce of civet, good apothecary, to sweeten my
imagination: there's money for thee.

GLOUCESTER: O, let me kiss that hand!

KING LEAR: Let me wipe it first; it smells of mortality.

GLOUCESTER: O ruin'd piece of nature! This great world
145   Shall so wear out to nought. Dost thou know me?

KING LEAR: I remember thine eyes well enough. Dost thou squiny
at me? No, do thy worst, blind Cupid! I'll not love. Read thou
this challenge; mark but the penning of it.

GLOUCESTER: Were all the letters suns, I could not see one.

wren even does it, and the small golden fly copulates in front of my eyes. Let copulation prosper! Because Gloucester's illegitimate son was kinder to his father than my legitimate daughters were to me. Go for it! Lust and promiscuity because I need soldiers. Look at that girl over there; she looks extremely chaste. She pursues virtue and shakes her head when she hears people talk about sex. Neither the polecat nor the lively horse have a stronger sexual appetite. They are beasts from the waist down, though they're women from the waist up. The gods possess them from the waist up—beneath the waist, they belong to the devil. There's hell and darkness. There's the infernal pit, burning, heat, foulness, destruction. Agh. Agh. Pah. Pah ok to change Give me an ounce of perfume, good apothecary, to sweeten my imagination! There's some money for you.

GLOUCESTER: *Oh, let me kiss his hand.*

KING LEAR: *Let me wipe it first. It smells of mortality!*

GLOUCESTER: *Oh, you ruined fragment of a man! This universe will end in nothingness! Do you know me?*

KING LEAR: *I remember your eyes well enough. Are you squinting at me? No, do your worst, blind Cupid! I won't love. Read this challenge. Take a look at the handwriting on it.*

GLOUCESTER: *Even if all the letters were suns, I wouldn't be able to see one.*

150   EDGAR: [Aside] I would not take this from report; it is,
       And my heart breaks at it.

KING LEAR: Read.

GLOUCESTER: What, with the case of eyes?

KING LEAR: O, ho, are you there with me? No eyes in your head, nor
155   no money in your purse? Your eyes are in a heavy case, your
       purse in a light; yet you see how this world goes.

GLOUCESTER: I see it feelingly.

KING LEAR: What, art mad? A man may see how this world goes
       with no eyes. Look with thine ears: see how yond justice rails
160   upon yond simple thief. Hark, in thine ear: change places; and,
       handy-dandy, which is the justice, which is the thief? Thou hast
       seen a farmer's dog bark at a beggar?

GLOUCESTER: Ay, sir.

KING LEAR: And the creature run from the cur? There thou mightst
165   behold the great image of authority: a dog's obeyed in office.
       Thou rascal beadle, hold thy bloody hand!
       Why dost thou lash that whore? Strip thine own back;
       Thou hotly lust'st to use her in that kind
       For which thou whipp'st her. The usurer hangs the cozener.
170   Through tatter'd clothes small vices do appear;
       Robes and furr'd gowns hide all. Plate sin with gold,
       And the strong lance of justice hurtless breaks:
       Arm it in rags, a pigmy's straw does pierce it.
       None does offend, none, I say, none; I'll able 'em:
175   Take that of me, my friend, who have the power
       To seal the accuser's lips. Get thee glass eyes;
       And like a scurvy politician, seem

EDGAR: I would not believe this if anybody had told me a[bout it. It's] true, and my heart breaks over it!

KING LEAR: Read.

GLOUCESTER: How, with my eye sockets?

KING LEAR: Oh, ho. Is that the way things are? No eyes in your head, and no money in your purse? Your eyes are in a sad condition, your purse is light, yet, you see how things go in this world.

GLOUCESTER: I see it by feeling it.

KING LEAR: What, are you mad? A man can see how this world works without eyes. Look with your ears! Look how justice punishes a common thief. Listen, with our ear: change places, and—take your choice—who stands for justice, and who is the thief? Have you seen a farmer's dog bark at a beggar?

GLOUCESTER: Yes, sir.

KING LEAR: And the person ran from the dog? There you can see an example of authority: the dog is obeyed, because he holds an official position. You rascally officer, stop your violence! Why do you strike that whore? Punish yourself! You lustfully long for the same thing you're whipping her for. The big villains hang the little thieves! The small crimes of poor people are always noticed, while fine robes and fur-lined gowns hide everything. Protect sin with gold armor, and the strong lance of justice will break without inflicting pain. Cover sin in rags, and a pigmy's weapon made of straw will pierce it. Nobody commits crimes, nobody, I say, nobody. I'll exempt everyone from guilt. Learn this from me, my friend. I have the power of a king to silence the accuser. Get yourself glass eyes, and, like an evil politician, pretend to see the

[handwritten margin note: rethinking social order]

223

To see the things thou dost not. Now, now, now, now:
Pull off my boots: harder, harder: so.

180 Eᴅɢᴀʀ: O, matter and impertinency mix'd! Reason in madness!

Kɪɴɢ Lᴇᴀʀ: If thou wilt weep my fortunes, take my eyes.
I know thee well enough; thy name is Gloucester:
Thou must be patient; we came crying hither:
Thou know'st, the first time that we smell the air,
185 We wawl and cry. I will preach to thee: mark.

Gʟᴏᴜᴄᴇsᴛᴇʀ: Alack, alack the day!

Kɪɴɢ Lᴇᴀʀ: When we are born, we cry that we are come
To this great stage of fools: this a good block;
It were a delicate stratagem, to shoe
190 A troop of horse with felt: I'll put 't in proof;
And when I have stol'n upon these sons-in-law,
Then, kill, kill, kill, kill, kill, kill!

[Enter a Gentleman, with Attendants]

Gᴇɴᴛʟᴇᴍᴀɴ: O, here he is: lay hand upon him. Sir,
Your most dear daughter—

195 Kɪɴɢ Lᴇᴀʀ: No rescue? What, a prisoner? I am even
The natural fool of fortune. Use me well;
You shall have ransom. Let me have surgeons;
I am cut to the brains.

Gᴇɴᴛʟᴇᴍᴀɴ: You shall have any thing.

200 Kɪɴɢ Lᴇᴀʀ: No seconds? all myself?
Why, this would make a man a man of salt,
To use his eyes for garden water-pots,
Ay, and laying autumn's dust.

224

*things you don't see. No, now, now, now: pull off my boots,
harder, harder. Like this.*

EDGAR: [Aside] *Oh, sense and nonsense mixed up! Reason in madness.*

KING LEAR: *If you want to cry over my misfortunes, take my eyes. I know
you well. Your name is Gloucester. You must be patient. We came into
this world crying. You know that the first time we smell the air, we
scream and cry. I will preach to you—listen.*

GLOUCESTER: *Alas, alas, the day.*

KING LEAR: *When we are born, we cry because we have entered this great
stage of fools. This is a nice tree-stump. It would be ingenious to shoe
a troop of horses with felt. I'll give it a try. And when I have crept up
on these son-in-laws—then Kill! Kill! Kill! Kill! Kill! Kill!*

[A Gentleman and Attendants enter]

GENTLEMAN: *Oh, here he is! Take a hold of him. Sir, your dearest
daughter—*

KING LEAR: *No rescue? What, a prisoner? I was born to have fortune play
tricks on me. Treat me well. You will receive ransom. Let me see a
doctor. My mind has been split!*

GENTLEMAN: *You will have anything.*

KING LEAR: *No supporters? Just myself? Well, this would make a man cry
salty tears, to have his eyes used for filling garden water-cans, yes,
and to help settle the autumn dust.*

GENTLEMAN: Good sir,—

205 KING LEAR: I will die bravely, like a bridegroom. What!
     I will be jovial: come, come; I am a king,
     My masters, know you that.

GENTLEMAN: You are a royal one, and we obey you.

KING LEAR: Then there's life in't. Nay, if you get it, you shall get it
210   with running. Sa, sa, sa, sa.
                              [Exit running; Attendants follow]

GENTLEMAN: A sight most pitiful in the meanest wretch,
     Past speaking of in a king! Thou hast one daughter,
     Who redeems nature from the general curse
     Which twain have brought her to.

215 EDGAR: Hail, gentle sir.

GENTLEMAN: Sir, speed you: what's your will?

EDGAR: Do you hear aught, sir, of a battle toward?

GENTLEMAN: Most sure and vulgar: every one hears that,
     Which can distinguish sound.

220 EDGAR: But, by your favour,
     How near's the other army?

GENTLEMAN: Near and on speedy foot; the main descry
     Stands on the hourly thought.

EDGAR: I thank you, sir: that's all.

GENTLEMAN: *Good sir—*

KING LEAR: *I will die bravely, like a neat bridegroom. What! I will be happy! Come on, come on! I am a king, masters, remember that.*

GENTLEMAN: *You are royalty, and we obey you.*

KING LEAR: *Then the situation isn't hopeless. And you shall have it. You shall have it by running for it. Sa, sa, sa, sa.*
> [He exits running; Attendants follow]

GENTLEMAN: *A pitiful sight in a common wretch, not to mention in a king. You have one daughter, who redeems nature from the universal curse your two other daughters have brought upon it.*

EDGAR: *Greetings, noble sir.*

GENTLEMAN: *Sir, be quick! What do you want?*

EDGAR: *Have you heard anything, sir, of an upcoming battle?*

GENTLEMAN: *Most certainly. It's common knowledge. Everyone has heard about it who can hear at all!*

EDGAR: *But, please tell me, how close is the other army?*

GENTLEMAN: *Close, and moving quickly. We expect to see the main part of the troops any hour.*

EDGAR: *I thank you, sir, that's all.*

225   GENTLEMAN: Though that the queen on special cause is here,
         Her army is moved on.

    EDGAR: I thank you, sir.

                           [Exit Gentleman]

    GLOUCESTER: You ever-gentle gods, take my breath from me:
         Let not my worser spirit tempt me again
230   To die before you please!

    EDGAR: Well pray you, father.

    GLOUCESTER: Now, good sir, what are you?

    EDGAR: A most poor man, made tame to fortune's blows;
         Who, by the art of known and feeling sorrows,
235   Am pregnant to good pity. Give me your hand,
         I'll lead you to some biding.

    GLOUCESTER: Hearty thanks:
         The bounty and the benison of heaven
         To boot, and boot!

    [Enter Oswald]

240   OSWALD: A proclaim'd prize! Most happy!
         That eyeless head of thine was first framed flesh
         To raise my fortunes. Thou old unhappy traitor,
         Briefly thyself remember: the sword is out
         That must destroy thee.

245   GLOUCESTER: Now let thy friendly hand
         Put strength enough to 't.   *[Edgar interposes]*

GENTLEMAN: *Though the queen is here for particular reasons, her army has moved on.*

EDGAR: *I thank you, sir.*

[Gentleman exits]

GLOUCESTER: *You gods who are always kind, take my breath from me when the time comes. Let not evil spirits tempt me again to die before you decide to end my life.*

EDGAR: *Nicely prayed, father.*

GLOUCESTER: *Now, good, sir, who are you?*

EDGAR: *A very poor man who has become accustomed to misfortune. Due to the experience of sorrow, I am inclined to pity others. Give me your hand, and I'll lead you to some lodging.*

GLOUCESTER: *Heartfelt thanks. May the generosity and the blessings of heaven compensate you further!*

[Oswald enters]

OSWALD: *A man with a prize on his head! Most lucky! That eyeless head of yours was conceived and born to make me fortunate! You old, unfortunate traitor! Quickly recall your sins! The sword has been drawn that will destroy you.*

GLOUCESTER: *Now put strength into the strike with your friendly hand!*
[Edgar interferes and comes to his father's defense]

OSWALD: Wherefore, bold peasant,
    Darest thou support a publish'd traitor? Hence;
    Lest that the infection of his fortune take
250   Like hold on thee. Let go his arm.

EDGAR: Chill not let go, zir, without vurther 'casion.

OSWALD: Let go, slave, or thou diest!

EDGAR: Good gentleman, go your gait, and let poor volk pass. An
    chud ha' bin zwaggered out of my life, 'twould not ha' bin zo
255   long as 'tis by a vortnight. Nay, come not near th' old man; keep
    out, che vor ye, or ise try whether your costard or my ballow be
    the harder: chill be plain with you.

OSWALD: Out, dunghill!

EDGAR: Chill pick your teeth, zir: come; no matter vor your foins.
                    [They fight, and Edgar knocks him down]

260 OSWALD: Slave, thou hast slain me: villain, take my purse:
    If ever thou wilt thrive, bury my body;
    And give the letters which thou find'st about me
    To Edmund earl of Gloucester; seek him out
    Upon the British party: O, untimely death!   *[Dies]*

265 EDGAR: I know thee well: a serviceable villain;
    As duteous to the vices of thy mistress
    As badness would desire.

GLOUCESTER: What, is he dead?

EDGAR: Sit you down, father; rest you
270   Let's see these pockets: the letters that he speaks of
    May be my friends. He's dead; I am only sorry
    He had no other death's-man. Let us see:

230

OSWALD: *You insolent peasant, how dare you help a proclaimed traitor! Go away, or your fate will be the same as his. Let go of his arm!*

EDGAR: *I will not let go, sir, without further explanation.*

OSWALD: *Let go, you slave, or you'll die!*

EDGAR: *Good gentleman, continue on your own way, and let poor folk pass. If I could have been bullied out of my life, I wouldn't have lasted two weeks. No, don't come near the old man. Keep away, I'm warning you, or I'll find out whether your head is harder than my stick! I mean it!*

OSWALD: *Get away, you dirty beggar!* [They fight]

EDGAR: *I'll pick your teeth out, sir! Come, I'm not afraid of our sword-thrusts!* [Oswald falls]

OSWALD: *Slave, you have killed me! Villain, take my purse! If you ever hope to advance in life, bury my body. And give the letters I have on me to Edmund, Earl of Gloucester. Find him among the English army. Oh, untimely death! Death!* [Oswald dies]

EDGAR: *I know you well. A corrupt villain, as obedient to the schemes of your mistress as wickedness would have it!*

GLOUCESTER: *What, is he dead?*

EDGAR: *Sit yourself down, father, and rest. Let's take a look at his pockets. The letters he mentioned may be useful to me. He's dead! I'm only sorry that he had no other executioner. Let's see. With your permission, wax! Don't blame us, good*

Leave, gentle wax; and, manners, blame us not:
To know our enemies' minds, we'd rip their hearts;
275   Their papers, is more lawful.

[Reads] 'Let our reciprocal vows be remembered. You have
many opportunities to cut him off: if your will want not, time and
place will be fruitfully offered. There is nothing done, if he return
the conqueror: then am I the prisoner, and his bed my goal; from the
280   loathed warmth whereof deliver me, and supply the place for your
labour. 'Your—wife, so I would say—
'Affectionate servant,

                                        'Goneril.'

O undistinguish'd space of woman's will!
285   A plot upon her virtuous husband's life;
And the exchange my brother! Here, in the sands,
Thee I'll rake up, the post unsanctified
Of murderous lechers: and in the mature time
With this ungracious paper strike the sight
290   Of the death practised duke: for him 'tis well
That of thy death and business I can tell.

GLOUCESTER: The king is mad: how stiff is my vile sense,
That I stand up, and have ingenious feeling
Of my huge sorrows! Better I were distract:
295   So should my thoughts be sever'd from my griefs,
And woes by wrong imaginations lose
The knowledge of themselves.   *[Drum afar off]*

EDGAR: Give me your hand:
Far off, methinks, I hear the beaten drum:
300   Come, father, I'll bestow you with a friend.

                                        [Exeunt]

manners! We'd tear out our enemies' hearts, in order to know their minds. It's more lawful to tear open their letters.

[He reads] "Let us remember our mutual vows. There'll be many chances to end his life. If you don't lack the will to do it, there'll be plenty of places and opportunities. We will have achieved nothing, if he comes home victorious. Then I'll be his prisoner, and his bed my jail. Save me from the loathed intimacy of his bed and take his place instead. Your—I want to say wife—affectionate lover,
                                                                Goneril."

Oh, limitless lust in women! A plot to end her virtuous husband's life. And my brother to replace him! Here, in the sands, I'll bury you! You detestable messenger of murderous lechers, and when the time is ripe, I'll show the wicked letter to the duke, whose death has been plotted. It will be good for him if I can report both our death and your scheme.

GLOUCESTER: The king is mad. How stubborn are my wicked senses that I can stand up and feel a sharp awareness of my huge sorrows. It would be better if I was mad! Then my thoughts would be cut off from my grief. My misery would be forgotten in wild delusions.   [Drums sound in the distance]

EDGAR: Give me your hand. I think I hear drums in the distance. Come, father, I'll lodge you with a friend.

[They exit]

SCENE VII

A tent in the French camp.
Lear on a bed asleep, soft music
playing; Gentleman, and others attending.

[Enter Cordelia, Kent, and Doctor]

CORDELIA: O thou good Kent, how shall I live and work,
    To match thy goodness? My life will be too short,
    And every measure fail me.

KENT: To be acknowledged, madam, is o'erpaid.
5   All my reports go with the modest truth;
    Nor more nor clipp'd, but so.

CORDELIA: Be better suited:
    These weeds are memories of those worser hours:
    I prithee, put them off.

10 KENT: Pardon me, dear madam;
    Yet to be known shortens my made intent:
    My boon I make it, that you know me not
    Till time and I think meet.

CORDELIA: Then be 't so, my good lord.
15   *[To the Doctor]*
    How does the king?

DOCTOR: Madam, sleeps still.

CORDELIA: O you kind gods,
    Cure this great breach in his abused nature!
20   The untuned and jarring senses, O, wind up
    Of this child-changed father!

SCENE VII

A tent in the French camp.
Lear In a bed asleep, soft music playing;
Gentleman and others attending.

[Cordelia, Kent, and Doctor enter]

CORDELIA: *Oh you good Kent. How can I live and work to live up to your goodness? My life is too short, and every attempt will fail.*

KENT: *To receive recognition for my services, madam, is to be overpaid. All my accounts accord with the truth, neither overstated nor understated.*

CORDELIA: *Dress yourself better. These clothes are a reminder of bad times. I beg you, take them off!*

KENT: *I am sorry, my dear madam. But to reveal myself right now would jeopardize my plans. I ask you as a special favor not to recognize me for who I am until I think the time is right.*

CORDELIA: *Then that's how it will be, my good lord.* [To the Doctor] *How is the king doing?*

DOCTOR: *Madam, he's still sleeping.*

CORDELIA: *Oh, you kind gods, cure this great rupture in his mistreated mind; repair the confused and disorderly senses of this childlike father.*

235

DOCTOR: So please your majesty
That we may wake the king: he hath slept long.

25 CORDELIA: Be govern'd by your knowledge, and proceed
I' the sway of your own will. Is he array'd?

GENTLEMAN: Ay, madam; in the heaviness of his sleep
We put fresh garments on him.

DOCTOR: Be by, good madam, when we do awake him;
I doubt not of his temperance.

30 CORDELIA: Very well.

DOCTOR: Please you, draw near. Louder the music there!

CORDELIA: O my dear father! Restoration hang
Thy medicine on my lips; and let this kiss
Repair those violent harms that my two sisters
35 Have in thy reverence made!

KENT: Kind and dear princess!

CORDELIA: Had you not been their father, these white flakes
Had challenged pity of them. Was this a face
To be opposed against the warring winds?
40 To stand against the deep dread-bolted thunder?
In the most terrible and nimble stroke
Of quick, cross lightning? to watch—poor perdu!—
With this thin helm? Mine enemy's dog,
Though he had bit me, should have stood that night
45 Against my fire; and wast thou fain, poor father,
To hovel thee with swine, and rogues forlorn,
In short and musty straw? Alack, alack!
'Tis wonder that thy life and wits at once
Had not concluded all. He wakes; speak to him.

DOCTOR: Your majesty, please allow that we wake up the king. He has slept long.

CORDELIA: Let your knowledge guide you and proceed as you see fit. Is he dressed?

GENTLEMAN: Yes, madam. While he was sleeping heavily, we put fresh clothes on him.

DOCTOR: Stand close, good madam, when we awaken him. I don't doubt that he'll be under control.

CORDELIA: Very well.

DOCTOR: Please come closer. Play the music louder.

CORDELIA: Oh, my dear father. May my lips bring healing, and may this kiss repair the violent damage my two sisters inflicted on your honor!

KENT: Kind, dear princess.

CORDELIA: Even if you had not been their father, this white hair should have demanded pity from them. Is this a face that should be subject to raging winds, face the horrid sounds of roaring thunderbolts, or endure terrible and quick strokes of lightning? To occupy such a dangerous place with only his hair for a helmet? My enemy's dog, even if he had bit me, would have been welcome to rest in front of my fire on a night like that. And you had to be thankful, poor father, for sharing a shed with pigs and wretched vagabonds? In scanty and musty straw? Alas, alas! It's a miracle that your life and your mind did not come to an end all together. He's waking up. Speak to him.

50   DOCTOR: Madam, do you; 'tis fittest.

CORDELIA: How does my royal lord? How fares your majesty?

KING LEAR: You do me wrong to take me out o' the grave:
      Thou art a soul in bliss; but I am bound
      Upon a wheel of fire, that mine own tears
55   Do scald like moulten lead.

CORDELIA: Sir, do you know me?

KING LEAR: You are a spirit, I know: when did you die?

CORDELIA: Still, still, far wide!

DOCTOR: He's scarce awake: let him alone awhile.

60   KING LEAR: Where have I been? Where am I? Fair daylight?
      I am mightily abused. I should e'en die with pity,
      To see another thus. I know not what to say.
      I will not swear these are my hands: let's see;
      I feel this pin prick. Would I were assured
65   Of my condition!

CORDELIA: O, look upon me, sir,
      And hold your hands in benediction o'er me:
      No, sir, you must not kneel.

KING LEAR: Pray, do not mock me:
70   I am a very foolish fond old man,
      Fourscore and upward, not an hour more nor less;
      And, to deal plainly,
      I fear I am not in my perfect mind.
      Methinks I should know you, and know this man;
75   Yet I am doubtful for I am mainly ignorant
      What place this is; and all the skill I have
      Remembers not these garments; nor I know not

238

DOCTOR: Madam, you speak to him. It's more fitting.

CORDELIA: How is my royal lord doing? How is your majesty?

KING LEAR: You do me wrong to take me out of the grave. You are a soul in heaven, but I have to undergo the punishments of hell and purgatory. My own tears burn like molten lead!

CORDELIA: Sir, do you know who I am?

KING LEAR: You are a spirit, I know. When did you die?

CORDELIA: His mind is still wandering.

DOCTOR: He's barely awake. Leave him alone for a while.

KING LEAR: Where have I been? Where am I? Bright daylight? I have been misled. I would die full of pity if I saw someone else like this. I don't know what to say. I can't say for sure that these are my hands. Let's see. I can feel this pinprick. I wish I knew for sure what is going on.

CORDELIA: Oh, look at me, sir. And hold your hands over me in blessing. No, sir, you mustn't kneel.

KING LEAR: Please, don't mock me. I'm a very foolish, silly old man, over eighty years old, not an hour more or less. And, to be honest, I am afraid I'm not in my right mind. I feel like I should know you and this man. Yet, I have my doubts because I have no idea where I am, and, no matter how much I try, I don't remember these clothes. I also don't know where I stayed last night. Don't laugh at me, but, as I am a man, I think this lady is my child Cordelia.

cordelia's presence brings madness

Where I did lodge last night. Do not laugh at me;
For, as I am a man, I think this lady
80   To be my child Cordelia.

CORDELIA: And so I am, I am.

KING LEAR: Be your tears wet? yes, faith. I pray, weep not:
If you have poison for me, I will drink it.
I know you do not love me; for your sisters
85   Have, as I do remember, done me wrong:
You have some cause, they have not.

CORDELIA: No cause, no cause.

KING LEAR: Am I in France?

KENT: In your own kingdom, sir.

90   KING LEAR: Do not abuse me.

DOCTOR: Be comforted, good madam: the great rage,
You see, is kill'd in him: and yet it is danger
To make him even o'er the time he has lost.
Desire him to go in; trouble him no more
95   Till further settling.

CORDELIA: Will 't please your highness walk?

KING LEAR: You must bear with me:
Pray you now, forget and forgive: I am old and foolish.
[Exeunt all but Kent and Gentleman]

GENTLEMAN: Holds it true, sir, that the Duke of Cornwall was so
100   slain?

KENT: Most certain, sir.

CORDELIA: *And so I am. I am.*

KING LEAR: *Are you crying? Yes, indeed. I beg you, don't cry. If you have poison for me, I'll drink it. I know you don't love me. I remember that your sisters have done me wrong. You have some cause for that. They don't.*

1. LOSS OF TRUST)

CORDELIA: *No cause. No cause.*

KING LEAR: *Am I in France?*

KENT: *In your own kingdom, sir.*

KING LEAR: *Don't deceive me!*

DOCTOR: *Take comfort, good madam. You see that the madness has left him. And yet it's dangerous to fill in the lost time in his memory. Ask him to go inside. Don't trouble him anymore, until his mind is more composed.*

CORDELIA: *Does your highness want to withdraw?*

KING LEAR: *You must bear with me. Please forgive and forget. I am old and foolish.*

[All except for Kent and Gentleman exit]

GENTLEMAN: *Is it true, sir, that the Duke of Cornwall was killed like that?*

KENT: *Most certainly, sir.*

GENTLEMAN: Who is conductor of his people?

KENT: As 'tis said, the bastard son of Gloucester.

105 GENTLEMAN: They say Edgar, his banished son, is with the Earl
of Kent in Germany.

KENT: Report is changeable. 'Tis time to look about; the powers of
the kingdom approach apace.

GENTLEMAN: The arbitrement is like to be bloody. Fare you well, sir.

[Exit]

110 KENT: My point and period will be throughly wrought,
Or well or ill, as this day's battle's fought.

[Exit]

GENTLEMAN: Who is leading his people?

KENT: They say Gloucester's illegitimate son.

GENTLEMAN: They say that Edgar, his banished son, is in Germany with the Earl of Kent.

KENT: Rumors change. It's time to be on guard. The British forces are approaching quickly.

GENTLEMAN: The decisive fight will probably be bloody. Farewell, sir.

[He exits]

KENT: The outcome and goal of my life will be decided for good or bad with this battle.   [Exit]

- lear understands no flattery + power can make aling any diff.

(4.6.158 - 59)

ACT V

SCENE I

The British camp, near Dover.

[Enter, with drum and colours, Edmund, Regan, Gentlemen, and Soldiers.]

EDMUND: Know of the duke if his last purpose hold,
    Or whether since he is advised by aught
    To change the course: he's full of alteration
    And self-reproving: bring his constant pleasure.
    [To a Gentleman, who goes out]

5   REGAN: Our sister's man is certainly miscarried.

EDMUND: 'Tis to be doubted, madam.

REGAN: Now, sweet lord,
    You know the goodness I intend upon you:
    Tell me—but truly—but then speak the truth,
10   Do you not love my sister?

EDMUND: In honour'd love.

REGAN: But have you never found my brother's way
    To the forfended place?

ACT V

SCENE I

The British camp near Dover.

[Edmund, Regan, Gentlemen, and Soldiers enter with drums and colors]

EDMUND: *Find out if the duke sticks to his last plan, or whether he has recently decided to change his course of action. He keeps changing his mind and criticizing himself. Bring me his final decision.* [To a Gentleman, who then leaves]

REGAN: *Our sister's steward has come to some harm.*

EDMUND: *I'm afraid that's the case.*

REGAN: *Now, my sweet lord, you know that I plan on doing you some good. Tell me, but truthfully and be honest, do you love my sister?*

EDMUND: *In an honorable way.*

REGAN: *But have you never taken what belongs to my brother-in-law?*

EDMUND: That thought abuses you.

15 REGAN: I am doubtful that you have been conjunct
   And bosom'd with her, as far as we call hers.

EDMUND: No, by mine honour, madam.

REGAN: I never shall endure her: dear my lord,
   Be not familiar with her.

20 EDMUND: Fear me not:—
   She and the duke her husband!

[Enter, with drum and colours, Albany, Goneril, and Soldiers]

GONERIL: *[Aside]* I had rather lose the battle than that sister
   Should loosen him and me.

ALBANY: Our very loving sister, well be-met.
25   Sir, this I hear; the king is come to his daughter,
   With others whom the rigor of our state
   Forced to cry out. Where I could not be honest,
   I never yet was valiant: for this business,
   It toucheth us, as France invades our land,
30   Not bolds the king, with others, whom, I fear,
   Most just and heavy causes make oppose.

EDMUND: Sir, you speak nobly.

REGAN: Why is this reason'd?

GONERIL: Combine together 'gainst the enemy;
35   For these domestic and particular broils
   Are not the question here.

EDMUND: *Such a thought dishonors you.*

REGAN: *I think you might have been intimate with her.*

EDMUND: *No, on my honor, madam.*

REGAN: *I would not be able to endure this. My dear lord, please don't be intimate with her.*

EDMUND: *Don't be afraid! Regan and her husband, the Duke of Albany, are here.*

[Albany, Goneril, and Soldiers enter with drums and banners]

GONERIL: [Aside] *I'd rather lose the battle than have my sister come between me and him.*

ALBANY: *Greetings, our very loving sister. Sir, this is what I've heard: The king has gone to his daughter with some other men who were forced to leave as a result of our harsh rule. I have never shown bravery for the sake of dishonorable actions. As far as this situation goes, it concerns us because the king of France is invading our country; it's not because he supports the king with others, who, so I fear, have good and profound reasons for their opposition.*

EDMUND: *Sir, you speak nobly.*

REGAN: *Why are we discussing this?*

GONERIL: *We must combine our armies against the enemy. Our personal family quarrels are not relevant.*

ALBANY: Let's then determine
     With the ancient of war on our proceedings.

EDMUND: I shall attend you presently at your tent.

40   REGAN: Sister, you'll go with us?

GONERIL: No.

REGAN: 'Tis most convenient; pray you, go with us.

GONERIL: *[Aside]* O, ho, I know the riddle.—I will go.

[As they are going out, enter Edgar disguised]

EDGAR: If e'er your grace had speech with man so poor,
45   Hear me one word.

ALBANY: I'll overtake you. Speak.
                    [Exeunt all but Albany and Edgar]

EDGAR: Before you fight the battle, ope this letter.
     If you have victory, let the trumpet sound
     For him that brought it: wretched though I seem,
50   I can produce a champion that will prove
     What is avouched there. If you miscarry,
     Your business of the world hath so an end,
     And machination ceases. Fortune love you.

ALBANY: Stay till I have read the letter.

55   EDGAR: I was forbid it.
     When time shall serve, let but the herald cry,
     And I'll appear again.

ALBANY: *Then let's plan our strategy with the help of experienced officers.*

EDMUND: *I will join you in your tent immediately.*

REGAN: *Sister, you'll come with us?*

GONERIL: *No.*

REGAN: *It would be appropriate. Please, come with us.*

GONERIL: [Aside] *Oh no, I know what you're up to. I'll go.*

[Edgar enters, disguised, as they are going out]

EDGAR: *If your Grace would be willing to speak to a man as poor as I am, may I have a word with you?*

ALBANY: [To the others] *I'll catch up with you.* [To Edgar] *Speak.*
                    [All exit, except for Albany and Edgar]

EDGAR: *Before you fight the battle, open this letter. If you are victorious, let the trumpet sound for the one who brought it to you. Even though I seem poor, I can provide a champion who will prove everything that is stated here. If you lose, your business in this world will be done, and everything will come to a halt. May good fortune be with you!*

ALBANY: *Stay, until I have read the letter.*

EDGAR: *I was forbidden to. When the time is right, just have a messenger sound the trumpet, and I will reappear.*

ALBANY: Why, fare thee well: I will o'erlook thy paper.

[Exit Edgar]

[Re-enter Edmund]

EDMUND: The enemy's in view; draw up your powers.
60   Here is the guess of their true strength and forces
        By diligent discovery; but your haste
        Is now urged on you.

ALBANY: We will greet the time.   *[Exit]*

EDMUND: To both these sisters have I sworn my love;
65   Each jealous of the other, as the stung
        Are of the adder. Which of them shall I take?
        Both? one? or neither? Neither can be enjoy'd,
        If both remain alive: to take the widow
        Exasperates, makes mad her sister Goneril;
70   And hardly shall I carry out my side,
        Her husband being alive. Now then we'll use
        His countenance for the battle; which being done,
        Let her who would be rid of him devise
        His speedy taking off. As for the mercy
75   Which he intends to Lear and to Cordelia,
        The battle done, and they within our power,
        Shall never see his pardon; for my state
        Stands on me to defend, not to debate.   *[Exit]*

ALBANY: *Well, goodbye. I will read through the letter.*

[Edgar exits]

[Edmund reenters]

EDMUND: *The enemy is in sight. Get your troops together! Here is an esti-
mate of their strength and their forces, furnished by our busy scouts,
but you must now act quickly.*

ALBANY: *We will be ready to do what is required.*   [Albany exits]

EDMUND: *I have sworn my love to both sisters. Each is suspicious of
the other, as those who've been bitten are of the snake. Which of
them shall I take? Both? One? Or Neither? I can enjoy neither
one of them if both of them remain alive. If I take the widow,
I will upset and enrage her sister Goneril. It will be difficult
to win my game if her husband is alive. For now, we'll use his
authority for the battle. Afterwards, whichever sister wants to
get rid of him arrange his murder. As for the mercy he intends
to show Lear and Cordelia, they'll never see his pardon, once the
battle is over and they're in our power. My situation requires
actions, not words.*

[Edmund exits]

SCENE II

A field between the two camps.

[Alarum within. Enter, with drum and colours, King Lear, Cordelia, and Soldiers, over the stage; and exeunt]

[Enter Edgar and Gloucester]

EDGAR: Here, father, take the shadow of this tree
    For your good host; pray that the right may thrive:
    If ever I return to you again,
    I'll bring you comfort.

5   GLOUCESTER: Grace go with you, sir!
                                          [Exit Edgar]

[Alarum and retreat within. Re-enter Edgar]

EDGAR: Away, old man; give me thy hand; away!
    King Lear hath lost, he and his daughter ta'en:
    Give me thy hand; come on.

GLOUCESTER: No farther, sir; a man may rot even here.

10   EDGAR: What, in ill thoughts again? Men must endure
    Their going hence, even as their coming hither;
    Ripeness is all: come on.

GLOUCESTER: And that's true too.   *[Exeunt]*

SCENE II

A field between the two camps.

[War noises are being heard. Lear, Cordelia, and Soldiers enter with drums and banners, cross the stage, and exit]

[Edgar and Gloucester enter]

EDGAR: *Here, father, seek shelter in the shadow of this tree. Pray that the right side wins! If I ever return to you, I'll bring you good news.*

GLOUCESTER: *May God be with you, sir.*

[Edgar exits]

[Sounds of troop advancement, then retreat. Edgar reenters]

EDGAR: *Come away, old man. Give me your hand; let's go. King Lear has lost; he and his daughter have been captured. Give me your hand; come on.*

GLOUCESTER: *No further, sir. A man can die here just as well.*

EDGAR: *What, you are having dark thoughts again? Men must endure their death in this world the way they must endure being born. The only thing that matters is to be ready. Come on.*

GLOUCESTER: *And that's true, too.*

[They exit]

SCENE III

The British camp near Dover.

[Enter, in conquest, with drum and colours, Edmund, King Lear and Cordelia, prisoners; Captain, Soldiers, etc.]

EDMUND: Some officers take them away: good guard,
    Until their greater pleasures first be known
    That are to censure them.

CORDELIA: We are not the first
5   Who, with best meaning, have incurr'd the worst.
    For thee, oppressed king, am I cast down;
    Myself could else out-frown false fortune's frown.
    Shall we not see these daughters and these sisters?

KING LEAR: No, no, no, no! Come, let's away to prison:
10 We two alone will sing like birds i' the cage:
    When thou dost ask me blessing, I'll kneel down,
    And ask of thee forgiveness: so we'll live,
    And pray, and sing, and tell old tales, and laugh
    At gilded butterflies, and hear poor rogues
15 Talk of court news; and we'll talk with them too,
    Who loses and who wins; who's in, who's out;
    And take upon's the mystery of things,
    As if we were God's spies: and we'll wear out,
    In a wall'd prison, packs and sects of great ones,
20 That ebb and flow by the moon.

EDMUND: Take them away.

KING LEAR: Upon such sacrifices, my Cordelia,
    The gods themselves throw incense. Have I caught thee?
    He that parts us shall bring a brand from heaven,
25 And fire us hence like foxes. Wipe thine eyes;
    The good-years shall devour them, flesh and fell,

SCENE III

The British camp near Dover.

[Edmund enters, as victor, with drums and banners; Lear, Cordelia, as prisoners; Captain, Soldiers]

EDMUND: *Some officers shall take them away. Guard them well until our powerful leaders have announced the judgment they will pass on them.*

CORDELIA: *We are not the first people who have to endure the worst, despite their good intentions. I am sad for you, my oppressed king. For myself, I could have conquered our bad fortunes. Will we not see these "daughters" and "sisters"?*

KING LEAR: *No, no, no, no. Come, let's go into prison. We two, alone, will sing like birds in a cage. When you ask me for my blessing, I'll kneel down and ask your forgiveness. This way, we'll live, and pray and sing and tell old stories and laugh at the fashionable people and hear poor rogues talk about the news from court. And we'll talk with them, too—whoever loses or wins, who's in and who's out. And we'll claim to understand the secrets of the world, as if we were spies sent down by the gods to watch over men. Within the prison walls, we'll outlast entire groups of political parties and factions, who come and go every month.*

EDMUND: *Take them away!*

KING LEAR: *Such sacrifices, my Cordelia are rewarded by the gods themselves. Have I caught you? Whoever wants to separate us will need a torch from heaven to drive us out of prison, as foxes are smoked out of their holes. Wipe away your tears! Their bodies*

Ere they shall make us weep: we'll see 'em starve first. Come.
   [Exeunt King Lear and Cordelia, guarded]

30   EDMUND: Come hither, captain; hark.
      Take thou this note; *[Giving a paper]* go follow them to prison:
      One step I have advanced thee; if thou dost
      As this instructs thee, thou dost make thy way
      To noble fortunes: know thou this, that men
35   Are as the time is: to be tender-minded
      Does not become a sword: thy great employment
      Will not bear question; either say thou'lt do 't,
      Or thrive by other means.

   CAPTAIN: I'll do 't, my lord.

40   EDMUND: About it; and write happy when thou hast done.
      Mark, I say, instantly; and carry it so
      As I have set it down.

   CAPTAIN: I cannot draw a cart, nor eat dried oats;
      If it be man's work, I'll do 't.   *[Exit]*

*[Flourish. Enter Albany, Goneril, Regan, another Captain, and
Soldiers]*

45   ALBANY: Sir, you have shown to-day your valiant strain,
      And fortune led you well: you have the captives
      That were the opposites of this day's strife:
      We do require them of you, so to use them
      As we shall find their merits and our safety
50   May equally determine.

   EDMUND: Sir, I thought it fit
      To send the old and miserable king
      To some retention and appointed guard;

256

will decay entirely, before they make us cry. We'll see them starve first! Come.

[Lear and Cordelia exit, guarded]

EDMUND: *Come here, captain, listen! Take this note and follow them to prison. I have already improved your position. If you follow these instructions, you will come to considerable wealth. Remember that men must take advantage of their opportunities. It does not become a soldier to be weak. Your assignment does not allow any discussion. Either say that you'll do it, or advance in some other way.*

CAPTAIN: *I'll do it, my lord.*

EDMUND: *Go ahead! And consider yourself lucky once you have completed it. Take note! Immediately! And do it exactly as I've instructed you to.*

CAPTAIN: *I cannot draw a cart like a horse or live on oats, but if it's man's work, I'll do it.*   [Captain exits]

[A trumpet sounds. Albany, Goneril, Regan, another Captain, and Soldiers enter]

ALBANY: *Sir, today you have demonstrated your brave qualities, and good fortune has guided you well. You have captured the enemies of today's battle. We ask you to turn them over, so that we can treat them as required by their deserts and our safety.*

EDMUND: *Sir, I decided it was appropriate to send the old and miserable king into guarded confinement. His age and his title have the power to draw the sympathy of the common people, and to turn our*

Whose age has charms in it, whose title more,
55 To pluck the common bosom on his side,
An turn our impress'd lances in our eyes
Which do command them. With him I sent the queen;
My reason all the same; and they are ready
To-morrow, or at further space, to appear
60 Where you shall hold your session. At this time
We sweat and bleed: the friend hath lost his friend;
And the best quarrels, in the heat, are cursed
By those that feel their sharpness:
The question of Cordelia and her father
65 Requires a fitter place.

ALBANY: Sir, by your patience,
I hold you but a subject of this war,
Not as a brother.

REGAN: That's as we list to grace him.
70 Methinks our pleasure might have been demanded,
Ere you had spoke so far. He led our powers;
Bore the commission of my place and person;
The which immediacy may well stand up,
And call itself your brother.

75 GONERIL: Not so hot:
In his own grace he doth exalt himself,
More than in your addition.

REGAN: In my rights,
By me invested, he compeers the best.

80 GONERIL: That were the most, if he should husband you.

REGAN: Jesters do oft prove prophets.

soldiers against us. I sent the queen with him for the same reason. They will be ready tomorrow, or any day after that, to appear wherever you intend to hold your trial. Right now, we are exhausted and wounded. A friend has lost a friend. Even the best causes in war are cursed, in the heat of passion, by those who feel the bitter consequences of battle. The case of Cordelia and her father requires a more appropriate place.

ALBANY: *Sir, if I may say so, I regard you as a subordinate in this war, not as an equal.*

REGAN: *It's up to us to determine that. I think you should have inquired about our opinion before you had said that much. He led our troops; he followed the authority of my high rank and person. Due to this close connection, he may well stand up and call himself your equal.*

GONERIL: *Not so fast! He distinguishes himself through his own qualities rather than through the honors you have conferred upon him.*

REGAN: *Through the rights I have endowed upon him, he becomes an equal to the best.*

GONERIL: *That would be most fully realized if he became your husband.*

REGAN: *Prophecies are often made in jest.*

GONERIL: Holla, holla!
That eye that told you so look'd but a-squint.

REGAN: Lady, I am not well; else I should answer
85   From a full-flowing stomach. General,
Take thou my soldiers, prisoners, patrimony;
Dispose of them, of me; the walls are thine:
Witness the world, that I create thee here
My lord and master.

90   GONERIL: Mean you to enjoy him?

ALBANY: The let-alone lies not in your good will.

EDMUND: Nor in thine, lord.

ALBANY: Half-blooded fellow, yes.

REGAN: *[To Edmund]* Let the drum strike, and prove my title thine.

95   ALBANY: Stay yet; hear reason. Edmund, I arrest thee
On capital treason; and, in thine attaint,
This gilded serpent *[Pointing to Goneril]*
For your claim, fair sister,
I bar it in the interest of my wife:
100   'Tis she is sub-contracted to this lord,
And I, her husband, contradict your bans.
If you will marry, make your loves to me,
My lady is bespoke.

GONERIL: An interlude!

105 ALBANY: Thou art arm'd, Gloucester: let the trumpet sound:
If none appear to prove upon thy head
Thy heinous, manifest, and many treasons,
There is my pledge; *[Throwing down a glove]*

260

GONERIL: *Holla, holla! The eye that sees this coming must suffer from distorted vision.*

REGAN: *Lady, I'm not feeling well. Otherwise I would give you my angry answer. General, take my soldiers, my prisoners, my inheritance. Do with them as you wish, and take me. My heart is yours. May the world be a witness as I make you here my lord and master.*

GONERIL: *Do you plan on marrying him?*

ALBANY: *You don't have the power to prevent it.*

EDMUND: *Nor do you, lord.*

ALBANY: *Bastard, yes, I do!*

REGAN: *[To Edmund] Let the drums sound and announces that I'll share my title with you.*

ALBANY: *Stay and listen to reason. Edmund, I arrest you for capitol treason, and, in connection with your impeachment, this deceptive serpent. [Pointing to Goneril] As for your claim, fair sister-in-law, I prohibit it in the interest of my wife. She has already been betrothed to this lord, and I, her husband, contradict your banns of marriage. If you must marry, prove your love to me. My lady is taken!*

GONERIL: *What a farce!*

ALBANY: *You are armed, Gloucester. Let the trumpet sound. If nobody appears to prove your horrible, profound, and manifold treason, here is my challenge [Throwing down a glove]! I'll prove it on your life,*

I'll prove it on thy heart,
110   Ere I taste bread, thou art in nothing less
Than I have here proclaim'd thee.

REGAN: Sick, O, sick!

GONERIL: *[Aside]* If not, I'll ne'er trust medicine.

EDMUND: There's my exchange: *[Throwing down a glove]* what in
          the world he is
115   That names me traitor, villain-like he lies:
Call by thy trumpet: he that dares approach,
On him, on you, who not? I will maintain
My truth and honour firmly.

ALBANY: A herald, ho!

120 EDMUND: A herald, ho, a herald!

ALBANY: Trust to thy single virtue; for thy soldiers,
All levied in my name, have in my name
Took their discharge.

REGAN: My sickness grows upon me.

125 ALBANY: She is not well; convey her to my tent.
                                  [Exit Regan, led]

[Enter a Herald]
    Come hither, herald,—Let the trumpet sound,
And read out this.

CAPTAIN: Sound, trumpet!   *[A trumpet sounds]*

before I eat another piece of bread, that you are in no detail of the charges less guilty than I have described!

REGAN: *Sick, oh I'm sick.*

GONERIL: [Aside] *If not, I'll never trust poison again.*

EDMUND: [Throwing down a glove] *Here is my answer: Whoever calls me a traitor lies like a villain. Let your trumpets sound. If anybody dares to approach, I will defend my honor against him, against you, against anybody.*

ALBANY: *A herald. Here.*

EDMUND: *A herald. Here. A herald.*

ALBANY: *Trust in your unaided valor! Your soldiers, all levied in my name, have been discharged by me.*

REGAN: *I am feeling sicker.*

ALBANY: *She is not feeling well. Take her to the tent.*
                              [Regan exits, with assistance]

[A Herald enters]
    Come here, herald! Let the trumpet sound! And read this.

CAPTAIN : *Sound the trumpet.*   [A trumpet sounds]

HERALD: *[Reads]* 'If any man of quality or degree within the lists of the
130   army will maintain upon Edmund, supposed Earl of Gloucester, that
he is a manifold traitor, let him appear by the third sound of the trumpet: he is bold in his defence.'

EDMUND: Sound!   *[First trumpet]*

HERALD: Again!   *[Second trumpet]*

135   HERALD: Again!   *[Third trumpet]*
                                            [Trumpet answers within]

[Enter Edgar, at the third sound, armed, with a trumpet before him]

ALBANY: Ask him his purposes, why he appears
    Upon this call o' the trumpet.

HERALD: What are you?
    Your name, your quality? and why you answer
140   This present summons?

EDGAR: Know, my name is lost;
    By treason's tooth bare-gnawn and canker-bit:
    Yet am I noble as the adversary
    I come to cope.

145   ALBANY: Which is that adversary?

EDGAR: What's he that speaks for Edmund Earl of Gloucester?

EDMUND: Himself: what say'st thou to him?

EDGAR: Draw thy sword,
    That, if my speech offend a noble heart,
150   Thy arm may do thee justice: here is mine.
    Behold, it is the privilege of mine honours,

264

HERALD: [Reads] *"If any man of quality or distinction enlisted in the army will claim that Edmund, the supposed Earl of Gloucester, is a traitor on several counts of treason, let him appear at the third sound of the trumpet. He will defend himself bravely."*

EDMUND: *Sound.*   [First trumpet sounds]

HERALD : *Again.*   [Second trumpet sounds]

HERALD: *Again.*   [Third trumpet sounds]
                    [Another trumpet is heard nearby.]

[Edgar enters, after the third sound, carrying a trumpet]

ALBANY: *Ask him what his purpose is for appearing upon this call of the trumpet.*

HERALD: *Who are you? Your name? Your rank? And why did you answer the call?*

EDGAR: *Please know that my name has been lost. Treason has devoured it. Yet, I am as noble as the adversary I've come to fight.*

ALBANY: *Who is that adversary?*

EDGAR: *Who speaks in the name of Edmund, Earl of Gloucester?*

EDMUND: *He himself! What do you have to say to him?*

EDGAR: *Draw your sword! If what I have said offends a noble heart, your bravery may avenge you. Here is mine. Behold: It is the privilege of my honorable rank, my oath, and my knighthood to draw it. I solemnly declare, in spite of your strength, youth, position,*

My oath, and my profession: I protest,
Maugre thy strength, youth, place, and eminence,
Despite thy victor sword and fire-new fortune,
155 Thy valour and thy heart, thou art a traitor;
False to thy gods, thy brother, and thy father;
Conspirant 'gainst this high-illustrious prince;
And, from the extremest upward of thy head
To the descent and dust below thy foot,
160 A most toad-spotted traitor. Say thou 'No,'
This sword, this arm, and my best spirits, are bent
To prove upon thy heart, whereto I speak,
Thou liest.

EDMUND: In wisdom I should ask thy name;
165 But, since thy outside looks so fair and warlike,
And that thy tongue some say of breeding breathes,
What safe and nicely I might well delay
By rule of knighthood, I disdain and spurn:
Back do I toss these treasons to thy head;
170 With the hell-hated lie o'erwhelm thy heart;
Which, for they yet glance by and scarcely bruise,
This sword of mine shall give them instant way,
Where they shall rest for ever. Trumpets, speak!
                    [Alarums. They fight. Edmund falls]

ALBANY: Save him, save him!

175 GONERIL: This is practise, Gloucester:
By the law of arms thou wast not bound to answer
An unknown opposite; thou art not vanquish'd,
But cozen'd and beguiled.

ALBANY: Shut your mouth, dame,
180 Or with this paper shall I stop it: Hold, sir:
Thou worse than any name, read thine own evil:
No tearing, lady: I perceive you know it.
                    [Gives the letter to Edmund]

and glory, despite your victory and your brand-new good fortune, despite your valor and your courage, that you are a traitor, deceitful to the gods, to your brother, and to your father. In conspiracy against this highly distinguished prince. From the top of your head to your lowest part and the dust beneath your feet, you are an infamous traitor. If you deny it, this sword, this arm, and my best intentions are prepared to prove to your heart, to which I speak, that you lie!

EDMUND: *It would be wise to ask for your name. But since you look so sincere and brave on the outside, and your speech reveals a trace of good breeding, I condemn and reject your claims, even though the rules of knighthood would allow me refuse your challenge. I throw these accusations of treason back at you and crush your heart with these hated lies. Since they barely brush and bruise your heart, my sword will give them an immediate passage and lay them to rest forever. Trumpets, sound.*

[They fight. Edmund falls]

ALBANY: *Save him. Save him.*

GONERIL: *This is trickery, Gloucester. By the rules of war, you were not obliged to fight an unknown antagonist. You have not been conquered, but cheated and deceived.*

ALBANY: *Shut your mouth, woman, or I will shut you up with this letter! Stop, sir! You're more evil than words can say! Read your own evil! You can't tear it up, lady; I can tell that you know what it says.*

GONERIL: Say, if I do, the laws are mine, not thine:
    Who can arraign me for 't.

185 ALBANY: Most monstrous! oh!
    Know'st thou this paper?

GONERIL: Ask me not what I know.   *[Exit]*

ALBANY: Go after her: she's desperate; govern her.

EDMUND: What you have charged me with, that have I done;
190   And more, much more; the time will bring it out:
    'Tis past, and so am I. But what art thou
    That hast this fortune on me? If thou 'rt noble,
    I do forgive thee.

EDGAR: Let's exchange charity.
195   I am no less in blood than thou art, Edmund;
    If more, the more thou hast wrong'd me.
    My name is Edgar, and thy father's son.
    The gods are just, and of our pleasant vices
    Make instruments to plague us:
200   The dark and vicious place where thee he got
    Cost him his eyes.

EDMUND: Thou hast spoken right, 'tis true;
    The wheel is come full circle: I am here.

ALBANY: Methought thy very gait did prophesy
205   A royal nobleness: I must embrace thee:
    Let sorrow split my heart, if ever I
    Did hate thee or thy father!

EDGAR: Worthy prince, I know't.

ALBANY: Where have you hid yourself?
210   How have you known the miseries of your father?

GONERIL: *What if I do? I make the laws, not you! Who can charge me for it?*

ALBANY: *How monstrous! Do you know this letter?*

GONERIL: *Don't ask me what I know.*   [Goneril exits]

ALBANY: *Follow her. She's desperate! Guard her!*

EDMUND: *I have done what you have charged me with—and more, much more. It will come out with time. It's in the past, and so am I.* [To Edgar] *But who are you, who has defeated me? If you are noble, I forgive you.*

EDGAR: *Let's be tolerant toward each other. I am no less noble than you are, Edmund. If more so, then you have wronged me even more. My name is Edgar, and I am your father's son. The gods are just. They use the vices we enjoy in order to punish us. His mistake of fathering you has cost him his eyes.*

EDMUND: *You have said it right. It's true. The wheel of fortune has turned all the way, and I am at the bottom.*

ALBANY: [To Edgar] *I thought that the way you carried yourself revealed a royal nobleness. I must embrace you. May sorrow punish me if I ever hated you or your father.*

EDGAR: *Worthy prince. I know this.*

ALBANY: *Where have you been hiding? How have you found out about your father's misery?*

EDGAR: By nursing them, my lord. List a brief tale;
　　　And when 'tis told, O, that my heart would burst!
　　　The bloody proclamation to escape,
　　　That follow'd me so near,—O, our lives' sweetness!
215　　That we the pain of death would hourly die
　　　Rather than die at once!—taught me to shift
　　　Into a madman's rags; to assume a semblance
　　　That very dogs disdain'd: and in this habit
　　　Met I my father with his bleeding rings,
220　　Their precious stones new lost: became his guide,
　　　Led him, begg'd for him, saved him from despair;
　　　Never,—O fault!—reveal'd myself unto him,
　　　Until some half-hour past, when I was arm'd:
　　　Not sure, though hoping, of this good success,
225　　I ask'd his blessing, and from first to last
　　　Told him my pilgrimage: but his flaw'd heart,
　　　Alack, too weak the conflict to support!
　　　'Twixt two extremes of passion, joy and grief,
　　　Burst smilingly.

230　EDMUND:　　　This speech of yours hath moved me,
　　　And shall perchance do good: but speak you on;
　　　You look as you had something more to say.

ALBANY: If there be more, more woeful, hold it in;
　　　For I am almost ready to dissolve,
235　　Hearing of this.

EDGAR: This would have seem'd a period
　　　To such as love not sorrow; but another,
　　　To amplify too much, would make much more,
　　　And top extremity.
240　　Whilst I was big in clamour came there in a man,
　　　Who, having seen me in my worst estate,
　　　Shunn'd my abhorr'd society; but then, finding
　　　Who 'twas that so endured, with his strong arms
　　　He fastened on my neck, and bellow'd out
245　　As he'd burst heaven; threw him on my father;

270

EDGAR: *I have nursed his sorrows, my lord. Listen to a brief story. And when I've told it, I fear my heart will burst! The death sentence that followed me—oh, how sweet our lives are! That we would suffer the pain of death hourly rather than die once and for all!—caused me to change into the clothes of a madman and to assume an appearance that even dogs ridiculed. Dressed like this, I met my father with his bleeding eye sockets, who had just lost their sight. I became his guide, led him, and begged for him, and saved him from despair. I never—oh what a mistake!—revealed my identity to him, until about half an hour ago, when I was wearing armor. Not sure, though hopeful, of a fortunate outcome, I asked for his blessing, and told him my story from beginning to end. But his fractured heart—alas!—too weak to endure the stress, torn between two emotional extremes, between joy and grief, broke in happiness.*

EDMUND: *Your speech has touched me and might do some good. Go on. You look as though you have more to say.*

ALBANY: *If there is something to say that's even sadder; keep it to yourself. I am about to cry, just hearing about this.*

EDGAR: *This must seem extremely sad to anyone who cannot deal with sorrow. To say more, and elaborate on it, would make it even worse and exceed the limits of grief. While I was crying loudly, a man came in, who, having seen me in my horrible condition, would have shunned my detestable presence. But when I revealed who I was and what I endured, he clasped me around my neck and cried out, as if to burst heaven. Then he threw his arms around my father and told the most pitiful tale about Lear and himself that anyone ever heard. While retelling it, his grief overpowered him, and his heart began to*

Told the most piteous tale of Lear and him
That ever ear received: which in recounting
His grief grew puissant and the strings of life
Began to crack: twice then the trumpets sounded,
250   And there I left him tranced.

ALBANY: But who was this?

EDGAR: Kent, sir, the banish'd Kent; who in disguise
Follow'd his enemy king, and did him service
Improper for a slave.

[Enter a Gentleman, with a bloody knife]

255   GENTLEMAN: Help, help, O, help!

EDGAR: What kind of help?

ALBANY: Speak, man.

EDGAR: What means that bloody knife?

GENTLEMAN: 'Tis hot, it smokes;
260   It came even from the heart of—O, she's dead!

ALBANY: Who dead? speak, man.

GENTLEMAN: Your lady, sir, your lady: and her sister
By her is poisoned; she hath confess'd it.

EDMUND: I was contracted to them both: all three
265   Now marry in an instant.

EDGAR: Here comes Kent.

fade. That's when the trumpets sounded twice, and I left him there unconscious.

ALBANY: *But who was this?*

EDGAR: *Kent, sir, the banished Kent. In disguise, he followed his angry king and served him in a way that would be too humble for a slave.*

[A Gentleman enters with a bloody knife]

GENTLEMAN: *Help, help, oh help!*

EDGAR: *What kind of help?*

ALBANY: *Speak, man!*

EDGAR: *What does this bloody knife mean?*

GENTLEMAN: *It's warm and steaming. It has just come out of the heart of—oh, she's dead!*

ALBANY: *Who's dead? Speak, man!*

GENTLEMAN: *Your lady, sir, your lady! And her sister has been poisoned by her. She has confessed it.*

EDMUND: *I was engaged to both of them. All three of us now marry at once.*

EDGAR: *Here comes Kent.*

ALBANY: Produce their bodies, be they alive or dead:
This judgment of the heavens, that makes us tremble,
Touches us not with pity.   *[Exit Gentleman]*

[Enter Kent]
270   O, is this he?
The time will not allow the compliment
Which very manners urges.

KENT: I am come
To bid my king and master aye good night:
275   Is he not here?

ALBANY: Great thing of us forgot!
Speak, Edmund, where's the king? and where's Cordelia?
See'st thou this object, Kent?
[The bodies of Goneril and Regan are brought in]

KENT: Alack, why thus?

280   EDMUND: Yet Edmund was beloved:
The one the other poison'd for my sake,
And after slew herself.

ALBANY: Even so. Cover their faces.

EDMUND: I pant for life: some good I mean to do,
285   Despite of mine own nature. Quickly send,
Be brief in it, to the castle; for my writ
Is on the life of Lear and on Cordelia:
Nay, send in time.

ALBANY: Run, run, O, run!

290   EDGAR: To who, my lord? Who hath the office? send
Thy token of reprieve.

ALBANY: *Bring the bodies here, whether they're dead or alive.*
                                    [Gentleman exits]
This heavenly judgment, even though it moves us, does not arouse our pity.

[Kent enters]
Oh, is it Kent? We don't have time for the ceremonious greeting that common courtesy demands.

KENT: *I have come to bid my king and master goodnight. Is he not here?*

ALBANY: *We have forgotten about it. Speak, Edmund. Where's the king? And where's Cordelia?* [The bodies of Goneril and Regan are brought in] *Do you see this spectacle, Kent?*

KENT: *Alas, why has this happened?*

EDMUND: *Still, Edmund was loved. One poisoned the other for my sake and killed herself afterwards.*

ALBANY: *Exactly. Cover their faces.*

EDMUND: *I long to live. I intend to do some good, in spite of my nature. Send someone to the castle quickly. Hurry! I have issued a warrant for the execution of Lear and Cordelia. Get there in time.*

ALBANY: *Run, run, oh, run!*

EDGAR: *To whom, my lord? Who is in charge? Send something indicating your pardon.*

EDMUND: Well thought on: take my sword,
    Give it the captain.

ALBANY: Haste thee, for thy life.   *[Exit Edgar]*

295 EDMUND: He hath commission from thy wife and me
    To hang Cordelia in the prison, and
    To lay the blame upon her own despair,
    That she fordid herself.

ALBANY: The gods defend her! Bear him hence awhile.
                          [Edmund is borne off]

[Re-enter King Lear, with Cordelia dead in his arms; Edgar, Captain, and others following]

300 KING LEAR: Howl, howl, howl, howl! O, you are men of stones:
    Had I your tongues and eyes, I'd use them so
    That heaven's vault should crack. She's gone for ever!
    I know when one is dead, and when one lives;
    She's dead as earth. Lend me a looking-glass;
305   If that her breath will mist or stain the stone,
    Why, then she lives.

KENT: Is this the promised end?

EDGAR: Or image of that horror?

ALBANY: Fall, and cease!

310 KING LEAR: This feather stirs; she lives! if it be so,
    It is a chance which does redeem all sorrows
    That ever I have felt.

KENT: *[Kneeling]* O my good master!

EDMUND: *Good idea. Take my sword and give it to the captain.*

ALBANY: *Run, on your life!*   [Edgar exits]

EDMUND: *He has orders from your wife and me to hang Cordelia in prison and to claim that she committed suicide out of despair.*

ALBANY: *May the gods defend her! Take him away for a while.*
                                    [Edmund is carried off]

[Lear enters, with Cordelia dead in his arms; Edgar, Captain, and others follow]

KING LEAR: *Howl, howl, howl, howl! Oh, you are men of stone! If I had your tongues and eyes, I would use them for lamenting and crying, until the heavenly roof cracks She's gone forever! I know when someone is dead and when someone is alive. She's as dead as earth! Lend me a mirror. If her breath will mist or stain it, she lives.*

KENT: *Is this the end of the world?*

EDGAR: *Or a likeness of that horror?*

ALBANY: *Let the earth come to its end!*

KING LEAR: *This feather stirs. She lives! If so, it will make up for all the sorrows I have ever felt.*

KENT: [Kneeling] *Oh, my good master.*

KING LEAR: Prithee, away.

315 EDGAR: 'Tis noble Kent, your friend.

KING LEAR: A plague upon you, murderers, traitors all!
    I might have saved her; now she's gone for ever!
    Cordelia, Cordelia! stay a little. Ha!
    What is't thou say'st? Her voice was ever soft,
320   Gentle, and low, an excellent thing in woman.
    I kill'd the slave that was a-hanging thee.

CAPTAIN: 'Tis true, my lords, he did.

KING LEAR: Did I not, fellow?
    I have seen the day, with my good biting falchion
325   I would have made them skip: I am old now,
    And these same crosses spoil me. Who are you?
    Mine eyes are not o' the best: I'll tell you straight.

KENT: If fortune brag of two she loved and hated,
    One of them we behold.

330 KING LEAR: This is a dull sight. Are you not Kent?

KENT: The same,
    Your servant Kent: Where is your servant Caius?

KING LEAR: He's a good fellow, I can tell you that;
    He'll strike, and quickly too: he's dead and rotten.

335 KENT: No, my good lord; I am the very man,—

KING LEAR: I'll see that straight.

KENT: That, from your first of difference and decay,
    Have follow'd your sad steps.

KING LEAR: *Please, go away.*

EDGAR: *It's the noble Kent, your friend.*

KING LEAR: *May sickness come over you, murderers, traitors, all of you! I might have saved her. Now she's gone forever. Cordelia, Cordelia! Stay a while! Ha! What is it you're saying? Her voice has always been soft, gentle, and low. An excellent thing in women. I killed the villain who hanged you.*

CAPTAIN: *Its true, my lords. He did.*

KING LEAR: *Did I not, fellow? I have seen days when, with my light sword, I would have made them jump. I am old now, and my afflictions bother me. Who are you? My eyes are not the best; I'll recognize you in a moment.*

KENT: *If fortune boasts of two people she most loved or most hated, we see one of them now.*

KING LEAR: *My eyes are truly failing. Aren't you Kent?*

KENT: *That's who I am. Your servant Kent. Where is your servant Caius?* [The name Kent used in disguise]

KING LEAR: *He's a good fellow, I can tell you that! He'll fight quickly. He's dead and decayed.*

KENT: *No, my good lord. I am the very man—*

KING LEAR: *I'll look into that right away.*

KENT: *I have followed your sad steps since your fortune began to change.*

279

KING LEAR: You are welcome hither.

340   KENT: Nor no man else: all's cheerless, dark, and deadly.
        Your eldest daughters have fordone them selves,
        And desperately are dead.

KING LEAR: Ay, so I think.

ALBANY: He knows not what he says: and vain it is
345   That we present us to him.

EDGAR: Very bootless.

[Enter a Captain]

CAPTAIN: Edmund is dead, my lord.

ALBANY: That's but a trifle here.
        You lords and noble friends, know our intent.
350   What comfort to this great decay may come
        Shall be applied: for us we will resign,
        During the life of this old majesty,
        To him our absolute power: *[To Edgar and Kent]* you, to your
                    rights:
        With boot, and such addition as your honours
355   Have more than merited. All friends shall taste
        The wages of their virtue, and all foes
        The cup of their deservings. O, see, see!

KING LEAR: And my poor fool is hang'd! No, no, no life!
        Why should a dog, a horse, a rat, have life,
360   And thou no breath at all? Thou'lt come no more,
        Never, never, never, never, never!
        Pray you, undo this button: thank you, sir.
        Do you see this? Look on her, look, her lips,
        Look there, look there!   *[Dies]*

KING LEAR: *You are welcome here.*

KENT: *No, neither I nor anyone else. Everything is cheerless, dark, and dead! Your eldest daughters have killed themselves out of despair.*

KING LEAR: *Yes, I think so.*

ALBANY: *He doesn't know what he's saying. There's no use in trying to explain everything to him.*

EDGAR: *Very useless.*

[A Captain enters]

CAPTAIN: *Edmund is dead, my lord.*

ALBANY: *That's of small importance here. Lords and noble friends, know our intentions. We will provide any comfort possible to this ruined, great man! As for us, we will resign our royal power to him for the remainder of his old majesty's life.* [To Edgar and Kent] *As for you, I want you to assume your rightful places with all the advantages and distinctions your honorable deeds deserve. All friends shall be rewarded for their goodness, and all enemies punished as they deserve. Oh, see, see!*

KING LEAR: *And my poor daughter has been hanged! No, no, no life. Why should a dog, a horse, a rat have life, and you're not breathing at all? You will not come back. Never, never, never, never, never! Please, undo this button. Thank you, sir. Do you see this? Look at her, look. Her lips, look there, look there!*

[Lear dies]

365   EDGAR: He faints! My lord, my lord!

KENT: Break, heart; I prithee, break!

EDGAR: Look up, my lord.

KENT: Vex not his ghost: O, let him pass! he hates him much
     That would upon the rack of this tough world
370   Stretch him out longer.

EDGAR: He is gone, indeed.

KENT: The wonder is, he hath endured so long:
     He but usurp'd his life.

ALBANY: Bear them from hence. Our present business
375   Is general woe. *[To Kent and Edgar]* Friends of my soul, you
          twain
     Rule in this realm, and the gored state sustain.

KENT: I have a journey, sir, shortly to go;
     My master calls me, I must not say no.

ALBANY: The weight of this sad time we must obey;
380   Speak what we feel, not what we ought to say.
     The oldest hath borne most: we that are young
     Shall never see so much, nor live so long.

[Exeunt, with a dead march]

EDGAR: *He's fainted! My lord, my lord!*

KENT: *Break, oh heart! I beg you, break!*

EDGAR: *Look up, my lord.*

KENT: *Don't anger his departing spirit. Oh, let him pass away. It would be hateful to prolong his suffering in this world.*

EDGAR: *He is gone, indeed!*

KENT: *It's a miracle that he has endured this long. He barely clung on to his life.*

ALBANY: *Carry them away. Our concern now is mourning.* [To Kent and Edgar] *Friends of my soul, you both shall rule this kingdom and uphold this country.*

KENT: *I have to go on a journey very soon. My master calls me, and I cannot refuse.*

ALBANY: *We must carry the weight of this sad time and speak what we feel, not what we should say. The oldest has suffered the most. We who are young will never see this much, nor grow this old.*

[They exit, accompanied by a death march]

Study Guide

Act I, Scene I
King Lear wants to divide his kingdom among his three daughters. What question does he ask his daughters, and why does he eventually banish Cordelia?

Act I, Scene II
Edmund forges a letter from his brother Edgar and shows it to his father. Why does Edmund deceive them both? Why does he seem to feel so much anger and resentment?

Act I, Scene III
What does Goneril complain about to her steward Oswald? What does she want Oswald to do?

Act I, Scene IV
King Lear is angry because he does not receive the respectful treatment he demands in Goneril's house. When the fool talks to Lear, his language is full of imagery. What does he criticize the king for?

Act I, Scene V
King Lear prepares for his departure to his daughter Regan's house. What does the fool predict about the king's plans?

Act II, Scene I
Edmund has been dissatisfied with his personal situation since the beginning of the play. How does Edmund manage to get rid of his brother Edgar?

Act II, Scene II
After a fight with Oswald, Kent is put in stocks by Cornwall and Regan. Why did he attack Oswald?

Act II, Scene III

What decision does Edgar make after he is forced into banishment by his father and brother?

Act II, Scene IV

At the end of this scene, King Lear leaves the house of Regan and ventures into the cold night. What causes him to become upset and angry with both of his daughters?

Act III, Scene I

What news does Kent convey to the Gentleman, and what favor does he ask of him?

Act III, Scene II

King Lear addresses the natural elements and exclaims, "I am a man more sinn'd against than sinning." Elaborate on his remark.

Act III, Scene III

Describe the exchange between Edmund and his father Gloucester. What are Edmund's intentions; what are Gloucester's?

Act III, Scene IV

King Lear meets Edgar, disguised as Poor Tom. As he begins his descent into madness, Lear compares himself with the poor beggar. Why does he see parallels between himself and Poor Tom? What does he think they have in common?

Act III, Scene V

Comment on Edmund's advancements in this scene.

Act III, Scene VI

When Edgar, disguised as Poor Tom, observes King Lear's imaginary trial, he learns a lesson about his own struggles in life. How does Edgar begin to understand the concept of human interaction in the world?

Act III, Scene VII

The Duke of Cornwall and Regan display extreme cruelty when they viciously blind the Earl of Gloucester. What does their act teach about the concept of loyalty?

Act IV, Scene I

Blinded and roaming the countryside, Gloucester is finally aware of his son Edgar's innocence. He exclaims, "As flies to wanton boys, are we to the gods; they kill us for their sport." Explain what Gloucester is trying to say.

Act IV, Scene II

Goneril claims that her husband, the Duke of Albany, is a coward, acting like a woman, while she herself displays the bravery of a man. What do Goneril's statements reveal about her attitude toward men? How are her actions different from her husband's?

Act IV, Scene III

Why does King Lear presumably refuse to see his daughter Cordelia?

Act IV, Scene IV

What do we learn about King Lear's madness?

Act IV, Scene V

What do we learn about the underlying motives behind Regan's and Goneril's actions?

Act IV, Scene VI

Edgar leads his father to the cliffs of Dover where Gloucester intends to end his life. Describe what happens when the two arrive there. Why does Gloucester not die? How is his attitude toward life changed?

Act IV, Scene VII

King Lear wakes up in the French camp under the supervision of a doctor. What happens when he sees Cordelia? Who does he take her for?

Act V, Scene I

As the war rages, Regan and Goneril fight jealously over the love of Edmund. What is Edmund's attitude to the sisters and what is his plan of action?

Act V, Scene II

Who is victorious in the war?

Act V, Scene III

Edmund attempts to assume power and authority after the end of the war. Who finally defeats him?

Insightful and Reader-Friendly, Yet Affordable

Prestwick House Literary Touchstone Classic Editions–
The Editions By Which All Others May Be Judged

Every *Prestwick House Literary Touchstone Classic* is enhanced with Reading Pointers for Sharper Insight to improve comprehension and provide insights that will help students recognize key themes, symbols, and plot complexities. In addition, each title includes a Glossary of the more difficult words and concepts.

For the Shakespeare titles, along with the Reading Pointers and Glossary, we include margin notes and various strategies to understanding the language of Shakespeare.

New titles are constantly being added; call or visit our website for current listing.

Special Educator's Discount – At Least

50% Off

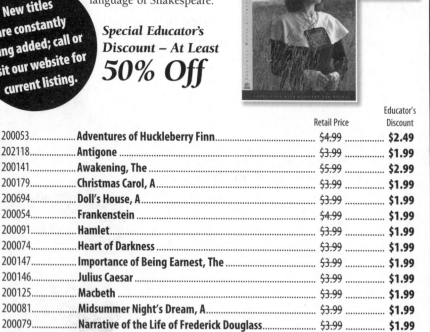